Bows Amidships

'Bowser! Midships!'

Bows Amidships

Bill Beavis

ADLARD COLES LIMITED
GRANADA PUBLISHING
London Toronto Sydney New York

Adlard Coles Ltd
Granada Publishing Ltd
8 Grafton Street, London W1X 3LA

First published in Great Britain by
Adlard Coles Ltd 1984

British Library Cataloguing in Publication Data
Beavis, Bill
    Bows amidships
    1. Shipping, Anecdotes, facetiae, satire etc.
    I. Title
    387.5   HE571

ISBN 0-229-11717-1

Typeset by Columns of Reading
Printed and bound in Great Britain by
Billing & Sons Ltd, Worcester

The author wishes to acknowledge his thanks to the editors of
Yachting Monthly and *Motor Boat and Yachting* for permission
to publish these items, most of which first appeared in these
magazines.

The Archetype

To a child the story of Noah is pure enchantment. It's only when you get a boat and a pet that you realise the immensity of that project.

In the great cabin of the *Ark* a very ancient man with a long white beard sat at a table cradling his head in his hands. He rocked slowly to and fro, moaning silently to himself. At his feet lay a large pile of parchment scrolls on which could be seen contour lines and compass bearings, and faces with their cheeks puffed out representing winds. These were the object of his distress.

'Oh *vey* . . . Oh *vey* . . . Fifty shekels – wasted,' he wailed. His eyes travelled once more down to the pristine scrolls. '*You're going on a long sea journey*, He says. So what do I do? I spend fifty shekels on a load of new charts! Then He says *I'm sending down a Flood. The sea is going to rise 15 cubits above the highest mountain tops, soundings, drying heights, depths, everything is going to change*! So NOW he tells me!'

He began to wail again. At that moment his tearful wife swept in.

'Noah! I got trouble.'

'Trouble? *Trouble*? Today I spend fifty shekels on charts where the mean sea level has got to be re-drawn, 50,000 feet higher; I got more corrections than flies round a camel and *you* got trouble. Do me a favour, Rachel.'

His wife, however, ignored his outburst and began to outline her problem.

'I got three snails coming up the gangway, and they all want to come aboard!'

'They know the rules. Two of each, a male and a female.' He picked up a scroll to begin the enormous task and turning to the table said helpfully, 'Tread on one, Rachel.'

'Yes, but *which* one? Snails are hermaphrodite.'

The old man looked puzzled. His wife suffered his incomprehension for a moment, then slapped her hand to her forehead.

'Have I got to explain *everything*? They don't have little boy snails and little girl snails, they're all the same. Ambidextrous, AC/DC, they don't have a determinate sex. They're hermaphrodite – they gotta be! The speed *they* move, they can't afford to be choosy.'

'So what matters?' shrugged Noah. 'Let 'em all aboard.' After a hundred years building the *Ark* he had a sympathy for slowcoaches. His wife was annoyed at what she saw was his sudden turn-around.

'So, we got the *big* heart now, eh? Different from yesterday when those nice couple of centaurs showed up.'

Noah, quick to defend yesterday's expulsion, produced a scrap of parchment from his pocket.

'No wonder it's taken so long.'

2

'He told me I wasn't to take half-humans. See, I got it written down – *No Hybrids*.' He sat back smugly.

'Oh, and what about those others you turned away?' she countered. 'Those pedigree dragons, for example. Then there was the Tritons, the Pans, the Pegasus and the Phoenixes, what's going to happen to them? I'll tell you what's going to happen to them. They're going to end up so much meat. Like those unicorns you stuck in with the lions. You're crazy! Just because they look good together on a coat of arms, that don't make them friends!'

'Listen, wife,' screamed Noah, his red face contrasting with the wispy whiteness of his hair. 'I'm a boatbuilder, not a ruddy vet! When He asked me to take this job on I didn't say, "Oh, that'll be nice, I'm interested in building an *Ark* with three decks, a big window and a ramp, so I can practise animal husbandry." I didn't say, "Oh goody-goody, boat-building's all right but what I've always *wanted* to do is run a zoo in the middle of the desert." '

At that moment there was a brilliant flash of light which fully illuminated the dark cabin. It was followed quickly by a loud retort and a slower, distant rumbling. On deck the elephants trumpeted with fear, lesser beasts howled and whined. Noah and his wife were stunned into silence and for a long while the old couple just looked at each other. Eventually Mrs Noah spoke.

'What was that?'

'How should I know? I've never been in a Flood before.'

Then it began to rain. The animals on deck got soaked. Then the wind got up and blew the rain in through the big window so the animals below got wet; the smell was unimaginable. It rained into pools which drained into rivulets which ran down the decks and began to fill up the bilges. It rained on the hill tops and it rained in the valleys, and soon the entire landscape began to disappear under a carpet of muddy, swirling water. And as the water rose so did the *Ark*. Her keel blocks bobbed up to the surface, and finally she was floating high above the land of Israel. But not for long; soon she was to be blown away by a terrible wind.

'I'll tell you one thing you've forgotten,' said Mrs Noah from under her sou'wester hat. 'You've forgotten to bring an anchor.'

'He didn't say anything about anchoring,' responded Noah, visibly shaken.

'Well, that's choice, that is. So what happens? I tell you what happens. We drift around forever is what happens. We get blown out across the oceans is what happens. We come to the edge of the world and we fall off is what happens. And all because you forgot to bring an anchor. By the way,' – she paused to wring out a sock – 'the dingoes have been asking when they can have their walkies.'

As the days wore on the privations of life aboard the *Ark* left their imprint on Mrs Noah. Not so much Noah himself, who had recently celebrated his 600th birthday. Diminishment of faculties had immunised him against much of the discomfort. The morning of the seventeenth day of the seventh month found Mrs Noah at the end of her patience. She awoke, dug her elbow into her sleeping partner's side and pulled up the hem of her nightie. 'You sure we've only got *two* fleas aboard?'

Noah turned a sleepy eye and was confronted with his wife's buttocks covered in red bumps and blotches. 'I've been scratching like mad all night.'

Noah conceded that living cheek by jowl, as he put it, with the world's entire stock of creepy-crawlies was not his preferred kind of cruising, the worst thing being that you daren't swipe or swot the things lest you knock out an entire species. He was about to tell her, by way of consolation, that only yesterday he had found a scorpion sleeping in his boot when there was a distinct scraping sound from

4

under the keel and the *Ark* came to rest. Noah immediately rushed up on deck, picked his way through the swishing tails, the bales of fodder and the droppings and came to the vessel's rail. Down through the water he could see the outline of rock.

'Is that *it*? Is that Mount Ararat?' asked his wife, who had joined him at the rail.

'Questions, questions – how do *I* know? I've never seen a mountain this way up before!'

Clear Moon, Frost Soon

Women's Work

When a man called up International Paints Ltd to complain that his two-pot polyurethane wouldn't set, their trouble-shooter was sent along to inspect it. Sure enough he found the paint completely uncured and asked if he could take the empty tins so that the residue could be examined in the laboratory.

5

The man said that was no trouble, opened up the boot of his Bentley, rooted about and eventually pulled out the tin of hardener – *unopened!* When it was explained that here was the mistake, that the two cans had to be mixed together to effect a chemical cure, the man began to get very agitated.

'*Damn* and *blast* the woman!' he said, slamming down the boot lid. 'Wait till I get hold of that secretary, it's *her* job to read the instructions!'

Tweet Tweet

A sailing friend, who is also an amateur bird-watcher, was puzzled by a call he hadn't heard before. Was it a marsh warbler? No, too regular for a marsh warbler. Could it be a sandpiper . . . or a curlew? There were some of each about. But no, it wasn't their usual cry; more of an alarm call, a steady squeak, squeak, which was now getting louder and louder. He laid down the glasses and looked around. A man on the sea-wall was coming towards him, pushing a rusty wheelbarrow.

At sea with falling glass
Soundly sleeps the careless ass

The Call Out

They knew a thing or two when they made me lifeboat crew *reserve*; during the entire six months we lived near the station I never once got there in time. I blame two factors: one, our house was outside the village at the bottom of a very steep hill; and two, instead of a car like everyone else, I only had a bicycle.

The fact that I would never go out in the lifeboat didn't stop me thinking that I might. And during this period I lived in a state of suspended animation, worried even about taking my clothes off at night. I was also very careful where I went. I didn't want an emergency catching me in the loft, or at the end of a very long ladder, or lounging in the bath. I developed an animal-like reaction to noise, always listening for the sound of maroons. Never in my life have I remained so tensed, so alert. Once when a lorry backfired I cleared cloth, plates and cutlery from a candlelit dinner.

The first call-out I missed was the morning after the Hockey Club dance. Too many drinks, rumbas and hokey-kokeys must have dulled my finely honed edge. My wife had to put me to bed. At 3 a.m. the maroons went off above the village. BOOM! BOOM! I thought they had gone off under the bed.

'*Quick*!' I shouted. 'What have you done with my clothes?' A lazy arm arched slowly across the bed and deposited my bow tie and dicky.

Outside, the bike was propped ready by the shed. I felt the tyres; they were good and hard. With my sleeve I wiped the rain off the saddle and then tried the running start I had been practising. But something went terribly wrong and instead of landing on the seat I forked down on the crossbar.

'What are you doing rolling about on the lawn?' asked a voice I recognised but could not see, her

7

torch focused on my pupils.

'I can't go, I'm hurt badly.'

'But you must go,' she said, pointing the torch out across the wind-driven sea. 'There is somebody out there depending on you.'

'Oh *sod* them,' I gasped. But the traditions of the lifeboats are instilled into every Englishman who lives by the sea and somehow I dragged myself up off the grass.

Cycling towards the village I could see stabs of car headlights illuminating the houses. Then occasionally the screech of tyres as another of the

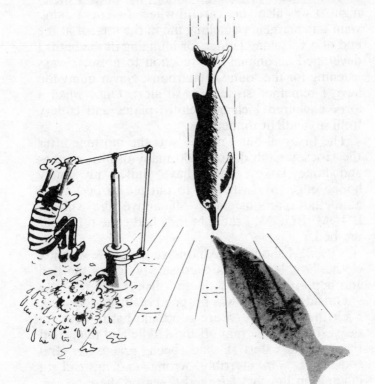

When the seahog jumps
Stand by your pumps

lifeboat's crew drove through the empty streets towards the harbour. Here and there a bathroom light could be seen and babies heard crying. Dogs disturbed by the sound continued now, barking in conversation. One dog I recognised lay quietly inside his gate waiting for his master to return. Would he ever return, I wondered. Would any of us?

I returned about five minutes later. The lifeboat had already left. I felt like a disgraced schoolboy; at that moment, missing the lifeboat seemed the most awful thing in the world. It was a feeling I would get used to. My wife would have gone back to bed and my main thought now was to get home quickly and reassure her that I was safe; we had only been married a year. I leaned the bike by the side of the shed ready for the next emergency and cooed softly through the letter box. Well, give her time to dry her eyes, I thought, when she failed to come to the door immediately. Ten minutes passed and I moved around to our bedroom window with a handful of gravel from the path. Little stones chipping against the window pane have romantic memories for us. But not this night obviously. I rang the bell, I hammered the door, I woke next door's chickens. None of these things aroused her.

Half a mile down the road there was a public telephone. A loud ringing alongside the bed would do the trick. The operator was very kind. I explained I was a lifeboatman with no small change; I didn't go into too much detail. She said she could ring the number. Finally, after what seemed an age, I heard my wife answer and the operator begin to speak.

'Will you accept a reverse-charge call from Yarmouth?' she asked.

'At four o'clock in the *morning*? Certainly not!' Then it clicked and the line went dead.

After that I always took my front-door key.

9

When clouds gather thick and fast
Keep sharp lookout for sail and mast

A Handful

I went to the fancy dress as Nelson. A blue raincoat pinned into tails made the frock coat, a pair of white combinations the trousers. Then just for fun, although at great discomfort, I wedged a tupperware bowl down the front for a codpiece.

You never know about people; towards the end of the evening a matronly lady came up to me, said how much she liked my codpiece and reached a hand down to grab it. I don't know who got the biggest shock. . .

I had taken it out half-an-hour before.

Over Paid?

If you had the misfortune to fall overboard from a square-rigged ship, your pay would be stopped immediately. You went off pay *the minute your feet left the deck*, almost as precise as a factory worker clocking off at the end of the day. With luck, they would throw you a lifebuoy, but the ship owner was loathe to provide these and, if you wanted any kind of buoyancy aid, you were supposed to bring your own.

My uncle fell overboard from a sailing ship in the middle of the Sargasso Sea. He said he was trying to grasp a handful of kelp which, so legend has it, would have won him the heart of a lady. (As it happened, he married my aunt.) Fortunately he fell over near the bow and, as the ship's progress was impeded by the weed, she was still alongside by the time he resurfaced and was able to clamber on board once again.

In all, he reckoned he wasn't gone more than three seconds. But they still logged him half a day's pay.

Disabled Tanker

An elderly lady in New Zealand, Mrs Amelia Pep, parked her invalid carriage on the life-boat ramp and promptly fell off to sleep. She slept so soundly that she didn't notice her chair inching forward nor, apparently, the water as it lapped over her feet. In a little while she was afloat. Fortunately, her carriage had a large fuel consumption and a correspondingly large tank. Fortunately, too, it was half empty and contributed sufficient buoyancy to keep the chair and Mrs Amelia Pep afloat until the lifeboat could be launched.

Heads you Lose

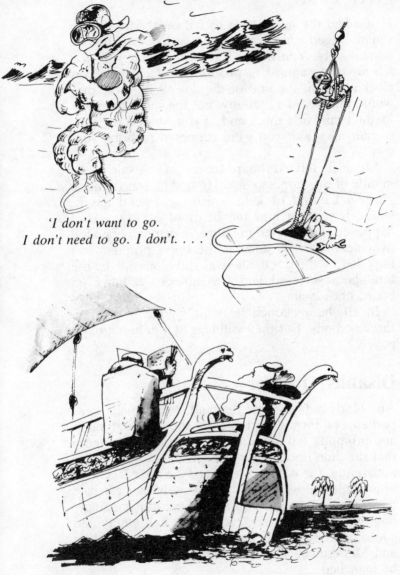

'I don't want to go.
I don't need to go. I don't. . . .'

'Hey Mustaph! I see the Dow Jones index
is up five points.'

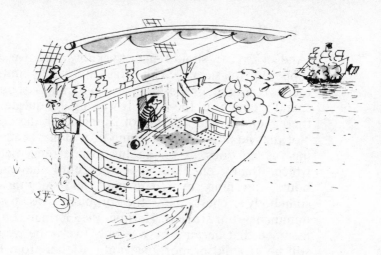

You can always fall back on the bucket

13

The Root Problem

'And *where*, I should like to know, are we all supposed to sleep?' This was my wife's initial reaction to the proposal that *two* families should spend the night in the boat. It was a good question; there were going to be ten of us including the dog. Not that he affects our sleeping provisions, preferring, as he does, to make his own arrangements which usually entail disappearing until the early hours, returning covered in mud, and sleeping on somebody's chest. No, the problem was more imminent – our student, Herman the German. I had assumed that because he was only twelve he would still be of child proportions, until a letter from his mother heralding his arrival informed us he was 'two metres long.'

'Can't we leave him behind with the dog?' I asked hopelessly.

'Don't be silly, he only knows about three words of English.'

'So does the dog. They should get along famously.'

'You had *no* business inviting the Browns in the first place. You *know* we've only got four beds.' It is always a useful resort in man-and-wife arguments if you can quickly aportion the blame.

'We have *eight berths*,' I corrected her. 'You are forgetting my root berths.'

 'You can't call those *awful* pull-out things beds,' she said. It is a timeless occupation on her part, disparagement of my root berths. It goes right back to the building days when I would sit up in bed, night after night, sewing them by the light of a candle. (I had to use a candle, since she'd tugged out the plug of my bedside light.)

Whether it was the fact that my sewing disturbed her – the flickering images, the rhythmic jingle of the bed springs, or the occasional spurts of blood – I

14

don't know, but she developed a dislike of the enterprise. On the other hand it could be Freudian. Maybe she sees the bed as the fountainhead of life, in which case my root berths must seem like a pauper's litter.

Not many boats *have* root berths these days, and since mine are an unorthodox design, then perhaps it might be helpful if I were to describe them. You don't see them immediately; they are hidden behind the backrest of each settee. They are large panels of canvas secured at their upper edge by a batten, while at the bottom edge is a sleeve, beautifully sewn, into which a pole is inserted. With this in place, the canvas can be stretched horizontal and the backrest cushion placed on top to give you instant double bunks – or *no* bunks, since in this instance I have neglected to mention the important stage of tying support ropes up to the deckhead. To prevent the root berth folding and closing on the incumbent like the jaws of a giant clam it is necessary to include a number of wooden struts beneath the mattress.

My wife objects mostly to the poles. They are not purpose-made, but items borrowed from around the boat. The mizzen boom, the sounding pole and the boathook all fit nicely. Her *bête noire* is the latter, which she says is menacing when sleeping underneath. But I find the big hook handy for hanging my watchstrap on.

'There's nothing for it,' announced my wife, when the Saturday came around. '*You* will have to sleep in your root berth.'

'Right then,' I said determinedly. 'Pass me that bottle of aspirins.' Getting into a root berth, for those who have never tried it, is like trying to post yourself between the upper bars of a farmyard gate. Nor is there any more room inside. Reading is out of the question, although I did manage to work out the washing instructions on my pyjamas. Given the

choice I like to sleep on my right-hand side, but
there was no choice and I lay pinioned on my back.
I watched the evening star go down; The Great
Bear come up; and contemplated that this could be
the longest night of my life.

'Bill, wake up.'

I tensed in the darkness, and here showed great
presence of mind. If I had sat up as one usually
does, I should have had a plywood collar around my
neck.

'What is it?' I enquired.

'I heard a *noise*.'

'Well, it's no good, I can't get out.' She fell silent
then – presumably ruminating over the misery of
climbing out of bed and looking around for herself.

'It's *all right*, it's gone now,' she said, thinking
better of it. You know, for an undisturbed night
there is a lot to be said for a root berth.

I'm thinking of fixing one to the bedroom ceiling
at home.

JACUZZI

Dial a Shanty

A lady reader wrote to ask if anyone in *Yachting
Monthly*'s office could put the tune to the words of
'*Eddystone Light*.' Somebody told her that I could,

and gave her my telephone number. One afternoon we were sitting down to tea when the telephone rang.

'That'll be your *mother*,' said my wife. 'She said she would call.' I went into the hallway to take the call which turned out to be the lady with the musical problem. I obliged by singing the four complete verses down the phone and went back to the tea table. My wife looked up.

'Why were you singing to your mother?'

Tight Fit

Troopships never did have a reputation for luxury, and in the American War of Independence particularly not. A contemporary document describes the conditions:

'The men were packed like herring. A tall man could not stand upright between the decks, nor sit up straight in his berth. To every such berth six men were allotted but, as there was room for only four, the last two had to squeeze in as best they might. Thus, the men lay "spoon fashion", and when they tired on one side, the man on the right would call "About face!" and the file would turn over at once;

17

then, when they were tired again, the man on the left would give the same order, and they would turn back to the first side.'

Next time your crew starts grumbling . . .

Hounded by Ghosts . . .

A good journalist always checks his facts, and so it was professionalism rather than disbelief which had me phoning round for details on this ghost. The bones of the story were that two friends of mine cruising the West Country had, by arrangement, picked up a private mooring at Kitley, at the head of the River Yealm. On their first night – which turned out to be their *only* night – they were awakened in the early hours by a man going past in a rowing boat shouting 'GEE-ORGE, GEE-ORGE!' in a weird, ethereal voice.

'Quick!' said the husband. 'Put out the *light*, we don't want any drunks aboard here!' Especially with weird ethereal voices. It wasn't a drunk though, as they could see when they looked, but a white, spook-like figure whose appearance made the hairs rise on the backs of their necks. They watched as the apparition rowed up and down a couple of times, still calling for the missing Gee-orge, before finally disappearing into the night.

Now, you would imagine that such bizarre and noisy goings-on would have been well known to the locals. However, when I telephoned Mr Anthony Maskell, who lives in a cottage overlooking the spot, and enquired whether he had seen a ghost, he laughed.

'When were they supposed to have seen this ghost?' he asked after I had retold the story.

'About 2 a.m. on 31st August,' I told him. Another blast of laughter.

'Well, I'm not too certain about the *time*,' he said, 'but the man in the boat that night was *me*!'

He explained that it was his custom, rowing back from the pub in the evening, to let his dog run down the river bank. This night, however, he was especially late, having stopped somewhere on the way, and the dog – who apparently does have a name but responds to the word DOG – failed to turn up at the rendezvous. It meant that his owner had to make several sorties up and down the river (in his white GRP simulated clinker boat) calling the animal.

Mr Maskell admits that after the first two runs his voice might have become a bit weird and ethereal.

Requiem for a Seagull

At about four o'clock on the afternoon of September 15 last year (I am certain of the date and time because the Insurance Claim Form is in front of me), I was sitting in the dinghy staring at some bubbles. The bubbles were coming from my outboard motor, still chugging away some two or three fathoms below me. Lack of air, the ingress of silt and the extreme damp would eventually get the better of it. But meanwhile it struggled on – stopping was never its strong point.

In the twenty-odd years we were together – 'ownership' is not a word I use – there was not a time I can remember the motor stopping as it was supposed to do. You had to use force. You had to tense yourself, then spring on it, throwing both arms around the flywheel, and hold tight for a couple of seconds. Owners of effete Japanese models would stare with stark horror.

'Hit the *stop* button!' they would shout.

'These models don't *have* a stop button,' I'd explain, then curse: I had relaxed my grip and the darned thing had started again.

Flywheel-hugging seemed to be the customary way of stopping the '52 model, although some

'E Berth. . . Step on it. Boat with a burst pipe.'

'I think we'll lay up here for the winter, Bert.'

'Yes, and it's going to save us hours re-caulking.'

Winter Sailing

'Alright machos, who's got my hot water bottle?'

owners reckoned to manage it by slapping their hand across the carburettor intake, which was trumpet-shaped for the purpose. Myself, I never learned that trick. I could introduce a muted tone, and could even slow the engine down to a heartbeat, but could never actually enforce total submission.

Still, the method of shutting down was unimportant. Far more to the point was the physical contact and the pleasant rapport which grew up between the Seagull engine and its owner. The modern outboard man must feel very little sense of involvement. A machine that stops and starts at the touch of a button, or never has to be coaxed, doesn't really *need* people. And how uninteresting they must be with everything hidden under a hood. No pipes to watch, no gaskets to examine for squirts, no in-cruise trouble-shooting or tinkering and, above all, nothing to kick. And where is the joy of unleashing power if you cannot actually *examine the response* – see all the parts chattering and whizzing round faster and faster? I suppose quietness does have its compensations: sometimes I did weary of shouting to the deaf-mute next to me. And probably it *is* very convenient to have an engine so well-behaved that you can leave it to look after itself . . . but where is your satisfaction? The old '52 Seagull gave you satisfaction, and more! It gave you status. You were not simply a driver – with a Seagull Forty you were a marine engineer!

Actually, I see from the Insurance Claim that mine was correctly called a Forty *Minus*. I never knew what the 'Minus' stood for, unless it could have meant minus clutch. Having no clutch gave the engine a projectile-like acceleration. Size for size, the Seagull Forty Minus could take off faster than anything on the water. To get under way, which was also the start procedure (when you haven't got a clutch it amounts to the same thing), it was necessary to open the throttle wide, with full choke. This, it was reasoned, gave sufficient reserves of rich fuel vapour to precipitate explosion should the spark prove too thin – a provision much respected by smokers. This also resulted in delivery of full revs to the propeller at the very instant that the engine fired. So with only a roar from the engine as warning, the boat would lunge forward into the tide, plucking from the pontoon any weak fittings, if you hadn't yet cast off. Unfortunately, getting under way was frequently a blind manoeuvre, since another requirement of the starting drill was to close the choke quickly before she stalled. And since this meant the driver couldn't also be expected to see where he was going, nobody ever got in the way of a '52 Seagull coming out from the bank . . .

There was a stubborn side to their nature. Very few of them fired first time. Both engine and owner knew this – it was understood. Most owners perfected their own starting drill, and it usually went something like this: after the first pull of the cord, which was just a preamble and nothing was expected to happen, you would try once more, then pretend to give up. Some people would even walk away, others would start whistling nonchalantly. My own ploy was to drag out oars and rowlocks and say, loudly and to no one in particular, 'She won't have it, no, she just *won't* have it,' then spring like a cat, yank the starter cord, and *bang!* you shocked her into life.

I can always tell a '52 Seagull owner. He looks fit. That was one thing these old engines certainly knew about, the importance of keeping their owners in trim. That starter cord, for example, it wasn't one of your decadent recoil types. You had to wind on, then *pull* . . . wind on, then *pull* . . . wind on, then *pull* . . . on bad days I've hand-cranked her all the way out to the mooring.

Still, I will say that in all those years she never let

me down when it mattered. I put it down to maintenance, which, in simple Seagull terms, meant looking after the plug and running her up in the dustbin for half an hour at the end of each season. People ask me if I will buy a Japanese model now that the old one is gone. Not likely! Not after I've seen that old Seagull shake my Japanese wristwatch into a thousand pieces.

No, I shall stick with my first love.

'Oh for heaven's sake, it can't be slowing us up that much.'

A Royal Gaffe

Two Yarmouth fishing smack skippers were deputed to present a model of a smack to Queen Victoria on behalf of the Mission to Deep Sea Fishermen. The following was the leading delegate's report to a meeting of his mates on his return:

'We went up to Buckin'ham Palace an' took that there model, an' when we got there, there was a feller met us dressed sech as yew never sawn an' he say to us, "Hev yew got that there model wot's for the Queen, together?"

'I say ter him, "Yis thet we heve," I say.

'So he say a me: "Cum yew along o' me then."

'Well, bor, we went threw room arter room an' at the finish we cum to a funny grit curtain, an' he say, "Stand yew here, an' when this here curtain is drawed to one side, dew yew go in," he say.

'Well, if yew believe me, I'd looked over thet there model an' went on lookin' over it a score o' times, an' I hent never sin nuthin' wrong with it. Then the curtain drawed to one side, an' there set the Queen, an' we made our obedience to har, an' I walked up a-holdin' of thet there model.

'An just afore I gan thet to har I looked down, an' blow me if the peak halyards worn't fast on the port side.'

'Whatever did the Queen say to that lot?' asked one of the fishermen, aghast at such an error.

'The Queen,' replied the old skipper, 'behaved like a perfect lady. She didn't pay no regard.'

Over a Barrel

The most remarkable thing about Guhajarat Singh was his unremarkability; he excelled in being ordinary, the man you never noticed the longest. Three months after he joined the ship people would stare as he loped by, then turn and swear that they had never seen him before.

Yet, in contradiction to all this, I noticed Guhajarat Singh the day he signed on in Calcutta. As each seaman made his thumb print – few could sign their names – it was my job to read their references. And I remember Guhajarat Singh's because his all read the same: 'Sober, honest, hardworking.' Every Chief Officer in every ship had made the identical comment. It was as if they couldn't remember the man and, rather than risk a libel, had simply copied the previous reference. It is doubtful that Guhajarat Singh knew the meaning of the words but he must have admired the repetitive symmetry for, unusually, his references were in pristine condition, kept in a box and tied with a ribbon.

The newly-joined crew must have been with us about two months when we were ordered to the South Pacific to load copra. Copra is the sun-dried fruit of the coconut and a slow cargo to load; you have to hop from port to port, picking up the harvest of each small island. It was, however, an ideal time to paint ship, and soon after arrival the Indian crew were given the preparatory job of chipping rust over-sides. In the still, dry weather the work progressed quickly and after a week or two of hammering and banging they had de-scaled the rust and finished the painting. Soon afterwards the loading was completed and we were on our way home after two long years.

Nothing could dampen the euphoria we felt the following morning, nosing northwards across the Pacific. Then, about 8 a.m., the carpenter came up on the bridge to say the ship was sinking. He had sounded Number 2 hold, and found six feet of water. The mate grabbed the engine-room phone and ordered the bilge to be pumped, then went off with the chippy to sound the hold again. An hour later and the level of water was still rising.

It was not difficult to guess how it happened. A war-built ship, substandard steel, somebody must have stuck their chipping hammer through the side. But explanations were irrelevant; the important thing was to find exactly *where* the hole was located. If we could determine this, then we could burrow through the copra and build a cement box around it.

Unfortunately, the mate went about things the wrong way psychologically. He should have said to the crew that all would be forgiven if the guilty man stepped forward and told exactly *where* he had put his hammer through the hull, instead of running down the foc'sle ranting and raving and swearing to tear the bastard's heart out. Naturally, it didn't get us anywhere.

All through the day, the tension built up as the level in the bilge grew higher. We had already changed course towards Port Moresby but it was touch and go whether we should reach there in time. That night as I lay in my bunk with a life jacket wedged under the pillow, my thoughts dwelling on this uncertain prospect, I suddenly heard footsteps on the deck above me, followed by a scraping sound as somebody took hold of the vent. A voice coming down a ventilator tube has an unearthly godly quality, and judging by the accent this was *Allah*:

'Apprentice Boy,' it began. Apprentices were often used as go-betweens for white officers and Indian crew.

'Yes,' I said, though I doubt that it was audible.

'It is me who is *making* hole in ship's side!'

I could think of no suitable answer, nor did it

matter for the voice then commanded me to fetch the Chief Mate and lock the door of my cabin. The mate nearly had a seizure when I explained there was a seaman with a message for him at my vent but he came. What else could he do?

'I am *telling* you where hole is,' began the voice once more.

'Good,' said the mate. 'Where is it? . . .'

'*But first* I am wanting something.'

There was a scraping sound within the vent shaft and we looked up to see a tin being lowered into the room. Inside was a sheaf of papers, references tied with ribbon. It was clear now what the man wanted. With great effort the mate picked up a pen, a sheet of our own ship's paper and began to copy the words.

'To my entire satisfaction. I have found Guhajarat Singh to be a sober, honest and hard-working seaman.'

Ladies' Charms Calm the Sea

Probably one of the most contrived old superstitions of the sea was that, in a storm, if a woman took off her clothes and stood up on deck her nakedness would calm the seas. No record survives of how the idea first started, but the Roman author Pliny (23-79 AD) recommends it along with other heavy-weather drills like battening down hatches or streaming warps. Fairly early in its career, however, the superstition changed character and the bare-breasted figurehead arrived – wives had got tired of whipping up their vests in the howling wind.

The figurehead soon developed a lore of its own, and one tradition which grew up was that the figure should never have ears. Sailors complained that ears fouled the ropes. You might imagine that a pair of large breasts would have been a greater hazard in this respect, but no.

Ears, they insisted, were the problem.

'That nice chemist from the Parade told me he was coming to Antigua this week.'

Fishy Business

A yachtsman anchored off Isla Contadora in the Bay of Panama, planning to take a trip ashore to the mainland. He used a Danforth anchor with plenty of nylon warp and, to be absolutely certain that it was holding, drove it in by running his engines astern for a full quarter of an hour. Satisfied that all was secure, he went ashore and took his plane to Panama City. Some ten hours later he returned to find that the boat had vanished. A man in a neighbouring boat told him he had seen it motoring away to the south and, when questioned about the possibility of theft, replied that he hadn't seen anyone aboard and had imagined that the owner was below with the boat on autopilot.

The owner hurriedly hired an aircraft and quite soon saw the boat, right on course, about 30 miles distant motoring slowly southwards. Then, as the plane came overhead, he could see that the boat wasn't under engine at all, but was evidently being towed. The anchor warp stretched out from the bow as taut as a fiddle string. At its end, he could see in the clear water a huge manta ray at least twelve feet across the wings. The creature was swimming along seemingly unperturbed with the stock of the 35-lb Danforth resting across the top of its head, and the flukes wedged under its chin.

FINGS ain't wot they used to be

When building a boat becomes the long and unremarkable affair that mine has been, it's only natural to put great store in small achievements. Insignificant though pencil racks, mug holders and carved nameboards may be in the grand scheme, they are for me important, being the only things I have to distinguish total stagnation from effort. If I *didn't* have these to exhibit to visitors, they might believe the high summer of today not much different from the spring of five years ago when I started.

So, understand the relevance of these and you will understand my disappointment when last month's contribution was rejected. . . .

I had just completed the children's bunks (begun long before as a single) and hoisted up my youngest to see them.

'Well, how do you think you'll like sleeping up here?' I enquired grandly, ignoring the run of diesel exhaust like the hotel manager who raptures over the magnificent view and dismisses the overhead railway. He considered the question in silence.

Finally he said, 'You *told* me there was going to be a garage.'

'Pardon?'

'You said that alongside the bed you would build a space for my Action Man Combat Vehicle.'

Even in my most solicitous moments I'm certain I never promised that. A matchbox toy maybe, or a little seat for Teddy, but an Action Man Combat Vehicle, never! Have you seen them? They're about the size of a Fiat 500 – but less manoeuvrable.

Young as he was, he typified my family's attitude. They have a high expectation of comfort. They don't distinguish between the essential and the frivolous. Compared to them the Victorian explorer with his jungle porters looks like an overnight tripper.

I tried to impress upon them that living on a boat required not only dealing with a very limited space, but also a change of *attitude*. Of course, life afloat is not without its compensations. What greater comfort can you enjoy than the soft glow of an oil lamp, or the warmth of an old stove with its fingers of woodsmoke filling every part of the cabin? I get quite lyrical thinking about it.

I love to describe conditions when I first went sailing, how after a long hard day I would snuggle

31

into the forecastle pipe cot with a stormsail drawn up over my head as protection from drips pinging down from the deckhead. What an atmosphere! Tinkling shackles above me, the ozone from the mud rising from the chain locker, the heady smell of Stockholm tar . . . in the morning the aroma of frying bacon and the steam drifting up from a mug of tea thoughtfully left for me on the lid of the toilet. That, I told my family, is the Joy of the Simple Life. 'That,' said my wife, 'is primitive!' and she went on to remind me what an awful state I would have drifted into if I hadn't married her.

All right, we have to accept a modicum of change if we want our families to come sailing. Action Man tanks, doll carriages, dimmer lights, cups with saucers, alright. But where do we draw the line?

'The *cloches* have arrived.'

'Pardon?' I climbed down the ladder to the ground to see my wife breaking open a packing case.

'Is that my anchor chain at last?' I asked hopefully.

'No. They don't usually pack anchor chain in straw and batting,' she said, passing me a handful. 'It's the cloches!'

I remembered then. We were down at the waterfront one morning when a man sailed in with lettuce growing under glass. (He said it was lettuce; it looked like marijuana.) My wife, who eats nothing out of a tin, said how wonderful it would be if we could grow our own salads. It *would* be wonderful. It would also be a biological miracle – she only plans to visit the boat every other weekend. Undeterred, she went ahead and ordered the little glass greenhouses and then climbed up the ladder onto the boat and chalked out a little vegetable garden – right where I planned to stand reefing the mainsail. I didn't say anything right away. Wasn't the mutiny on the *Bounty* sparked by someone heaving old Captain Bligh's breadfruit plants overboard?

As a matter of fact, I'm not against the idea of growing our own food. I mean, self-sufficiency is a very fine thing, but hardly conducive to happy living in a limited space. I can see us in the future up to our knees in chicken manure whispering sweet nothings to infant tomato plants with solar panels to port, sea-water distillers to starboard, and enough windmills aloft to fill a Van Gogh landscape.

I once saw a boat-sized sauna bath advertised. That could be a lot of fun: *'Suddenly, the squall struck as the unprepared boat heeled, and the sea swept aboard. In the steamy darkness of his pine-wood hell, Captain Courageous skipped over the flying hot stones, swearing as he grabbed for his towel.'*

We decided against the portable television in favour of a set of drums. I suggested that a wine

'Do you realise, Elsie, those silly fools are paying up to £8 a night in there!'

33

rack would be a little impractical, although the bidet remained a possibility for some time. We agreed on the four folding bikes, which defeated my idea for a walk-in sail locker. There's compensation, though. With the bikes out of the way, I have room to develop my film in the saloon.

As launching approached, relatives stopped by to unload their bits and pieces. We acquired a Japanese dinner service, a Canaletto print, an egg timer, ten leather-bound volumes of the *Encyclopaedia Britannica* and a battery vacuum cleaner. I'll find room for them somehow. I have to. No more thoughts of the simple life. In fact, you haven't seen such a sell-out of valuable space since Huckleberry Finn offered Tom Sawyer a bed in his drainpipe.

Proof that the Goodwin Sands do move was given when a German submarine, sunk in 1917, broke surface nearly sixty years later. For years she had been classed as a *Foul Area*; now she is a *Dangerous Wreck*.

Hernias were a common problem in sailing ships when men would strain at heaving ropes. Equally common was the cure. Men would climb aloft, secure their feet and hang upside down for a quarter of an hour.

A windsurfer was ordered out of the water by a Bermudian Police patrol for 'failing to keep his vessel in seamanlike order'. The police sergeant complained that the man did not have his regulation anchor, 10 ft of chain, warp, two oars and a lifebuoy.

Out of Season

Two brothers, one a horseman and the other a yachtsman, were arguing. The horseman said:

'I have a horse which costs less than a car, that I ride twice a week and which, when I'm not riding, manures my garden and trims my lawn. You have a boat which costs more than a house and demands more to maintain than an opera star. And you only use it one month in twelve!'

To which the yachtsman replied, 'Not so! I use her right through the year!'

'How's that?' asked the horseman.

'I dream of her.'

Knot Quite Right

I would not pretend that writing carries the same responsibilities as a proper job – publican, politician, lollipop man, general . . . even lollipop general. Nonetheless, it can have its worries. Last month, for example, I had a call from a publisher to inform me that a drawing I had done for a book of knots some ten years ago was wrong.

'Do you realise that people all over the world might be tying Spanish Bowlines incorrectly?' the editor droned. It was hard to take him seriously; of what possible consequence could it be? Besides, everyone knows that publishing is an area notorious for its errors.

'Tell me,' I countered, 'if this knot is so important, then why has it taken ten years for anyone to make a protest?' That had him. I could practically hear his brain ticking. On this triumphant note, I was about to put the phone down when his answer came.

'That's because dead men never complain.'

It was a day or two after this that I started having these nightmares . . .

*   *   *   *

On a narrow track over the Khyber Pass, a weary column of men are picking their way home.

35

*'I don't like it, Chief. That dredger's been gone
sixteen hours dumping her sludge.'*

Suddenly from the rear, a corporal sprints up and addresses the Colonel:

'Mr Maitland's compliments, Sir,' gushes the corporal. 'He's been shot. Doesn't want to hold the chaps up. Would you mind awfully finishing him off.' He hands the Colonel a pistol.

'Good God, man!' screams the Colonel. 'Can't waste valuable ammunition. Quick, in my pack – a copy of *Modern Rope Seamanship*! Bring a rope and we'll lower him into the valley.'

The sun is high by the time they reach the injured subaltern propped against a rock. They carry the man to the south face, safe from the home-made Afghani bullets, and prepare to secure him with the rope.

'Right, Smithers, read out the instructions on page 25 which describes the Spanish Bowline.' The corporal clears his throat and begins:

'This knot can be used to make a Bosun's Chair. Take the end of the rope and make three loops, as shown. Now pick up the left-hand loop A and pass this over loop B to join loop C . . . .' At this point the casualty becomes agitated and makes a grab for the book. The Colonel restrains him.

'Steady, man, we'll soon have you out of this mess.' He sticks a cheroot between his lips.

All goes well to begin with. They lower the injured man over the edge. Then suddenly he complains that the lower loop – the one under his buttocks – has begun to tighten at the expense of the upper loop around his chest. This constricture continues until his voice is whittled down to a throttling sound and the whole arrangement capsizes. The rope goes loose, there is a string of profanities, a long drawn out cry and then *thump*.

'I didn't quite catch that,' says the Colonel cranking his head.

'He said, Sir,' replies the corporal, that 'loop A should have gone *under* loop B.'

* * * *

William Darling is squinting through the rain-splattered glass and out to the distant rocks. As the beam from the lighthouse revolves he can just make out the swaying masts and shredded canvas that confirm his worst fears. He races down the winding stairs to where his daughter is sleeping. Her face is nestled against her teddy bear and a moment of tenderness overcomes him. What cruel fate, he reflects, to be born a lighthouse-keeper's daughter.

'Grace! Wake up! There's a ship on the rocks and you must help me take the boat.' The girl sits up and rubs her eyes.

'But what about Mama?'

'Your mother says it's your turn.'

Down in the cove, Grace can just make out their tiny boat riding to its buoy. In the lantern light it looks like a miniature ghost ship against the blackened sky. She is still trying to undo the endless whip that will haul the coble into the shore when her father arrives carrying the oars.

'What's delaying you, girl?' he asks.

'Mama's been practising knots from that book

again,' she pouts. William Darling drops to his knees to inspect the intractable mess. 'Looks like a Spanish Bowline,' he says. Then, later, 'Well, that's put the kybosh on that.' Together, father and daughter walk slowly back up the rocky path to the lighthouse. They reach the door then turn to look out on the angry sea. Finally, the father speaks.

'Y'know, Grace, if we had got out tonight, you might have gone down in history.'

* * * *

Thirteen days out of Alexandria, and the captain considers they have made good progress. After all the irritations and delays the weather, at least, has been generous. But tonight, things could be different – they will clear Cape St Vincent and be open to the North Atlantic. It is rather late in the year. For the moment, however, the sky is clear. He secretly crosses his fingers, says goodnight to the third mate and disappears to his cabin.

Lying on his bunk with a whisky in his hand, the captain reflects on the valuable cargoes he has

'And I still say the phase modulating diode was over-amplified.'

carried in the past. But this is the ultimate. How had the man from the British Museum put it?

'You've got a *priceless* cargo there, Captain. Look after it.' Well, he would do that all right. And on that quiet note of determination he finishes his drink, places it on his bunkshelf and drops off to sleep. Hours later he wakes to the sound of breaking glass.

'The *tow*! You've lost the tow!' he screams in disbelief as he staggers onto the bridge.

'Yes,' replies the mate sheepishly. 'We were just coming down to tell you.'

'But how, *how*?' He grasps the wheelhouse table and hangs there shaking his head. 'One hundred and eighty tons of Aswan granite, ordered at the hand of Rameses himself, one of the most valuable examples of ancient Egyptian culture! Cleopatra's Needle! And you've *lost* it! How, in hell's name,

'Funny thing, I don't think that was there when we started.'

how?' Not two inches from his finger tips, there, on the table, lies his answer: *Modern Rope Seamanship*. He picks it up in disgust.

'Not a Spanish Bowline,' he howls, 'you didn't make it fast with a Spanish Bowline?'

'No,' says the mate, 'we knew about the Spanish Bowline. This one was on the next page!'

Anyone can make a mistake

On 8th September 1923, a column of American destroyers, steaming at full speed in fog, made a tragic navigational error and crashed on to rocks known as the Devil's Jaw. Seven ships were totally wrecked and several more were crippled. Of the thirteen defendants who faced court martial on charges of negligence, two later became battleship captains, one was made a Commodore and two rose to Admiral.

Double-ender

The 'Kil' class were the strangest ships ever seen. Used in the battle against submarines in 1917, they were built as double-enders. With one funnel, one mast, two wheelhouses and a raised bow and stern, it was impossible to tell which way they were heading. And that, evidently, was the trick. For it was hoped that the U-boat skipper would be so confused that, rather than risk a torpedo firing off in the wrong direction, he would surface to face the ship's hidden guns.

Polar Bearings

Remarkably, on several occasions between 1682 and 1843 when the winters were exceptionally cold and the Arctic ice expansive, Eskimoes who had lost their bearings turned up in Scotland having paddled their kayaks all the way from Greenland.

Blue Salt Seller

The Atlantic has 3.6% salt, and so does the Caribbean. The Mediterranean, however, has 3.8% which is said to be why it is more blue.

Tall Ship Story

The *Dar Pomorza, Tovarisch* and *Kruzenshtern, Sagres II* and *Eagle*, owned respectively by Poland, Russia, Portugal and the United States, each have features in common; they are all huge Sail Training ships; they each take part in the Tall Ship races, were all built by Blohm and Voss and were each claimed as war reparations by the allies.

Tribal Marriages

During World War I, two destroyers of the early Tribal Class were damaged within the same week. The *Nubian* had her bow blown off and the *Zulu* was severely damaged at the stern. To save time and expense, ship repairers joined the two good halves together and *HMS Zubian* was created.

After the court enquiry, *Mary Celeste*, the mystery ship, was renamed and put up for sale. But while there might have been willing buyers, willing crews were hard to find. Over the next twelve years she was renamed and resold seventeen times. She was finally wrecked in a fraudulent insurance claim.

Reptiles' names for ships are unlucky. The Royal Navy has lost four *Vipers*, four *Serpents*, three *Lizards*, two *Snakes*, an *Adder*, a *Crocodile*, and a *Cobra*.

In 1840, the Mexican Navy acquired two steam frigates, the *Guadaloupe* and *Montezuma*. They

'So anyway, after Brixton I decided to come here for some peace and quiet.'

were the fastest, most formidable units on the American continent and, indeed, upset the balance of power. So proud was the Mexican Navy of these ships that when war broke out in the United States in 1846, they were promptly laid up, lest they should come to any harm.

Only one problem marred the excitement which surrounded the delivery of Argentina's new aircraft carrier in the 1950s. Who should enjoy the prestige of flying the planes, the air force or the yet-to-be-formed naval air wing? When a decision favoured the navy, tempers flared and air force pilots took off to bomb the carrier.

During the French Wars, the Navy had a ship the *Terrible* fitting out in Execution Dock. When an officer named Death was found on the active list, the association was too good to resist and he was placed in command. The joke was further compounded when a Lieutenant Spirit was unearthed and also sent to join, to be followed shortly by a surgeon called Ghost and a gunnery officer called Devil. To complete the macabre arrangements, the ship was given a skeleton as a figurehead. After a short and bitter engagement, she was captured by the French.

Many captains have given their names to stretches of land, such as Cook, Freemantle and Flinders. But none has been immortalised in quite the same way as Captain Corry. A conscientious man, he ordered a survey of the land when his ship anchored off Port Mudros in 1902. Lt Lockyer, the navigating officer, had been looking forward to going ashore to shoot partridges and was very much put out by this. So much so, that he decided to have his revenge.

It can still be seen today. On British Admiralty Chart No. 1662, there is a range of four small hills running down to Kombi Point. The names which Lt Lockyer gave them are Yam, Yrroc, Eb and Denmad. Turn these back to front and they spell the eternal message – May Corry Be Damned.

Superstition amongst sailors had become so strong and such a threat to discipline in the 19th century that the Royal Navy were determined to debunk it. They named a ship *HMS Friday*, found an officer named Friday to command her, launched on a Friday and sent her away on her maiden voyage on Friday 13th. She sank, of course.

The Cunard Shipping Line traditionally chose names for their ships which ended in *ia* and, after such successful and well-known ships as the *Mauretania* and *Aquitania*, this became their trade mark. In the 1930s they planned their biggest ship yet, to

The Red Sea Charter

'I remember now, Corporal Higgins and me came
here in a tank. . .'

'Me STARBOARD TACK. You savee starboard tack?'

'My boys make sail just one hour, you and memsahib
maybe one hour quarter.'

'Oh, never mind when it last happened,
let's get out of here!'

45

be named the *Victoria*. Then somebody pointed out that as the lady had been his grandmother they ought first to get permission from the King. Accordingly the directors approached His Majesty to explain that they wished to name the ship after Britain's noblest Queen.

'Fine,' said the King, 'I'm sure Her Majesty will be thrilled.'

Which is how Victoria came to be called the *Queen Mary*.

In the Beginning . . .

There is no record of when the first boat was built but it was probably in the earliest days of mankind's development. Driven by the need to fish, explore, trade and transport himself, we can safely conclude that Neanderthal Man built the first boat . . . and that Neanderthal Woman had a pretty big say in it.

On the leafy ground which now makes up the oil-rich reserves of the Forties Field, a hairy figure sat hunched over a stone tablet. His concentration was intense. His deep-set eyes scanned the imprint while a grubby finger traced over the lines. Slowly and with difficulty he read: *Log Boat Building for the Beginner*. He savoured the thought for a moment. Then, clapping one hand over the top of his squat head and hugging himself with the other, he breathed, 'Oh boy, oh *boy!*'

He went on saying those two words over and over again while he rocked to and fro, and dreamed of the places he would visit. So consumed was he that he hardly noticed evening arrive and the first specks of rain.

It was dark by the time he reached the cave. His wife met him at the entrance. She seemed to be in some distress; her two long arms were crooked behind her.

'What's up?' he asked at length.

'It's these new *brassières*,' she moaned. 'The fasteners get caught in me fur.'

'You should grumble,' he said, tugging at the white band under his chin. 'They make us wear collars at work and it's another 10,000 years before we develop a neck!' He brightened then as he remembered the stone slab he was carrying on his head.

'What you got there?' asked his wife eagerly, scuttling across the floor of the cave. 'Is it the plans for my kitchen extension?'

'No, it's a boat I'm going to build.'

She took the stone and moved toward the fire. Her small brow matted into a frown as she studied it at arms' length, holding it first vertically, then horizontally, then finally upside-down.

'Well, what d'you think?' he said at last.

'I *think*', she said, 'you won't be seeing me out in *that*,' and flung the stone to the ground.

Sleep did not come easy that night. Twice he had to get out of bed to hurl his boot at a sabre-tooth tiger howling round the dustbins. But the major cause of insomnia was thinking about his future boat. What voyages they would make! Already he could see the slender bow cleaving its way through the water, hear the rattling of the wash, the slow rhythmic splosh of the paddle and the feel of soft bark between his knees. Pity about the woman; still, nothing that a good clubbing couldn't sort out. And with that cosy thought, he finally slept.

'Yes, but how many people do *you* know who it's happened to?' he challenged when the subject came up at breakfast. She breathed a weary sigh, selected a nut with her delicate foot and popped it into her mouth.

'You near about it every day,' she said, munching. 'People who know nothing about the water, with no training, go out in these logs, and the next

47

thing, some plesiosaurus swims underneath and bites their leg off.'

He was about to bat her with his club but paused; there was something in what she said. Boating wasn't much fun with both legs trailing in the water. What was needed was a hollow shape, he pondered. And it so happened, by one of those strange circumstantial events which have marked the progress of mankind, that at that precise moment, *there*, in front of him, lay the solution – an earthenware porridge bowl.

'*Yeah!*' he exclaimed, when the significance of this finally got through. 'I'll make it like a porridge bowl.'

It took a lot of know-how to throw, heat and fire a 14-foot porridge bowl and our story moves on some years. But, finally, it was finished and when the first winter snows of that year had frozen into ice (and ice was becoming an increasing problem) he was able to slide his earthenware boat down to the river and push her afloat.

'Right then, we'll re-work it and this time call it longitude.'

'She don't look too seaworthy to me,' observed his wife, who had bought a new hat for the occasion. And, to the small audience which had assembled, she explained her misgivings about clay boat-building in the pre-Archimedes era. She was right, of course. The boat sank. He said it was because of her fidgeting.

'Look,' she explained on the first day of spring, when they finally got talking again, 'there was nothing wrong with your idea, but you were using the *wrong* material. Why don't you try some lightweight stuff, like sticks and skins?' The cloud that had darkened his brow for months suddenly lifted like a curtain. Chortling and cooing, he romped across the cave and sidled up alongside her.

'Who's a clever girl then?' he whispered, putting two long arms around her.

That last summer was a fine one. With the light which the long evenings brought into the cave, he was able to work extra hard at his new design. His wife was moderately enthusiastic. During the day she helped him cut down the willows and saplings that he then bent into the shape of a frame. Animal skins were harder to find. Dinosaurs were disappearing – everybody said so. But she did have extraordinary stealth and one day came whooping out of the trees to bag a couple of startled and very rare brontosauruses. It was just enough to finish the boat.

Naturally, she made demands. ('You don't get this sort of help for nothing.') The *Coracle*, the name they had chosen, had many female touches. A spacious and separate toilet compartment; a divided accommodation for the kids, plus a couple of large spaces earmarked for his fishing kit.

The first week of the cruise went wonderfully and, while her insistence that they eat fresh, wholesome food (which meant bringing the chickens, the pig and the goat) did cause some inconvenience, and the children's toys and pets, and her shoregoing clothes, spare shoes and make-up all helped to take the edge off the boat's performance, on the whole it was a great success.

But not the second week. It rained a lot, snowed

even more and, hanging around belowdecks, she grew moody and morose. Her discontent was finally voiced one evening after supper.

'When are you going to do something about this *roof*?'

'Pardon me?'

'This roof. It's too low. You seem to think that just because we're fresh out of the trees we're gonna always be bent up like a couple of crank handles! Look, I'm getting straighter every day.' She stood up to her full height and pointedly stuck her head through the thatch.

'How tall are you now, then?'

'Three feet and seven inches,' she answered proudly.

'Well, we can soon do something about that,' he said, reaching for his club.

Paddy of Post Office Bay

At Post Office Bay on the Galapagos Islands there is, or used to be, a mail barrel. The crews of

American whalers originally erected the barrel to deposit their letters for collection by homeward-bound ships. The custom still survives amongst cruising yachtsmen, although I am not certain that the original barrel does.

Anyway, the point of mentioning it is to introduce an Irish castaway called Pat Watkins, who lived alone on the island for five years – which, incidentally, makes him the longest domiciled castaway on record. Unhappily, the experience drove him mad and whalermen coming ashore with their letters would suddenly be jumped upon by this screaming Irishman with a long red beard and wild frightening eyes. So far as Watkins was concerned, this must have been a self-defeating exercise since his whole object of receiving the crews was to beg for bottles of rum. However, despite the hostile reception the crews gladly supplied his need, if only to make him absent himself for a couple of days and leave the post box in peace.

But drunk or sober, the attractions of life alone on the island must have been few, and clearly the daily round of finding food and water, making

'I do hope you're not in a hurry.'

51

shelters, building fires and jumping out on people was getting him down.

He decided to *take* a companion. Seeing a negro alone on the beach one day, who had been left to guard the longboat, he moved noiselessly with bare feet through the sand, crept up and pressed the trumpet rim of his musket against the man's head. Thus the negro had but little choice, and was kept in servitude for several years through dependence on Pat for food and water. Unbelievably, the madman recruited four more companions during his

stay and, either through fear or the sheer force of his personality, was able to subordinate them completely.

He became something of a nuisance internationally when, later, he began to smash up any boat which attempted to land on the island. Eventually warships were alerted but, with the uncanny instinct of a man who has gone bananas, he had already decided to leave the island and sail with his five followers to Guayaquil on the mainland. He was, however, the only one of the six to complete this voyage. The others all perished on the way.

In Guayaquil he fell in love and, after looking at tortoises for five years, we might guess that was an occasion more remarkable for its suddenness than its selectivity. Love was a new sensation and each night the castaway and his woman would be seen strolling through the old Spanish town. And with eyes that had sent a thousand terrified whalermen fleeing back to their boats, and leathery gums that could rip a cork from a bottle, he would smile and describe the paradise home that was awaiting her at Post Office Bay. Unhappily, the girl was denied this dream when one night the authorities bundled him into prison and threw away the key.

In familiarisation sessions aboard Sail Training Ships new crews are required to put on a safety harness and climb the foremast. This always results in confusion and boys generally seem to take longer to put on their harness than they do to climb the mast. Watch Officers have to sort out straps and buckles. But not so with the girl crews, who invariably pick up the harness without hesitation, shake it free and buckle it on without any bother.

'It's our *brassière* training,' explained one young thing.

So there you are. If you want to practise your

safety harness routine, just slip into your wife's bra now and then.

My dog was swimming in a gravel pit when he was struck from behind by a boat. Dazed, and limited by his particularly large turning circle, by the time he got around the boat had sailed away. The only nearby shipping that he *could* see was a small model-kit warship.

'Good God!' said a voice next to me, as the noise of crumpling plastic crackled across the water. 'Your dog's just sunk the *Bismarck*.'

The world's first underwater hotel has opened in Florida. A converted laboratory, it can take just two guests at 230 dollars a day. Travel is by submarine and guests will need to make a 'wet' transfer via a pressurized compartment.

That should stop them pinching the towels.

The easiest way to launder clothes in a boat is to wait until you are at anchor. Then pile the items into a plastic bucket with some water and detergent, seal the lid and suspend this from the bow. The action of

54

the sea rising and falling provides all the gentle agitation you need and in an hour or so they are clean.

Advice to sea-going cooks, from Richard B. Strout: 'Carry spaghetti instead of macaroni. Spaghetti is easily inspected for bugs, with macaroni you have to blow down the holes.'

Of Mice and Men

Nature works in strange and wondrous ways. When I fell to thinking about the ideal sailing companion I decided it should be somebody of simple tastes. Not a competitive type at home in a crowd but a modest soul who enjoys the peace and quiet you find in a boat. Well it seems I have now found those qualities exactly – in a mouse!

He must have come aboard last Friday. I noticed it shining in the morning sunlight, a little black dropping, plumb in the middle of the afterdeck.

Robinson Crusoe, confronted with that footprint in the sand, couldn't have been more startled. How did it get there? (Funny how you find yourself scanning the sky.) Ashore, the boat's deck stands a good seven feet above the ground and the ladder had been locked in the shed.

He must have come over the bow. He must have run along the top of the side fence, made a death-defying leap for the bobstay chain (death-defying because the dog's kennel is just underneath), heaved himself on to the bowsprit, padded away on the bow roller for a bit until he noticed the trees weren't flashing past, and finally shot off down the afterdeck. Remarkably agile – I wonder if I can train him to retrieve halyards?

Now, some people view the arrival of mice with horror, an indictment of their hygiene. I don't see it like that. I feel some sort of sympathy; a bond, even. After all, this mouse and I appear to have a lot in common. Both of us have wintered in the same house, with two wild stampeding kids, a tormenting dog and a wife who practises Spanish gypsy dancing (me, thankfully, above the ground, him beneath the floorboards). We're both refugees of a kind, boat people breaking away from a noisy, hostile world. The only difference between us is that if he did come over the bow like I described then he must be in much better shape than me.

Considering the available food supply, he won't be in good shape for long, in fact he'll have to be a pretty resilient mouse. I don't know how long he thinks he can last on a diet of Dunlopillo mattress and fibre-glass. He won't find any nice big hunks of canvas and cordage to munch, no traditional mouse fare.

To tell the truth I'm not crazy about mice and he's not exactly the kind of shipmate I would have chosen. On the other hand I do admit his presence does make a difference. I don't have that feeling of

total isolation. Another heart is beating. A sense of sharing, too. When I start up the sander and the dust flies, there's two pairs of lungs complaining, two pairs of hands clamping over two sets of ears when the air-cooled diesel is running.

But there is also embarrassment. Since nobody ever used to see me working in the boat, I adopted some quaint habits. For example, by wearing my wife's high-heeled sandals, I can just paint the deckhead without stretching; her headscarf is also useful. But with a mouse in residence I have to admit some discomfort; somewhere, a pair of eyes is quizzing me, a little nose twitching uncertainly, wondering who this middle-aged transvestite is.

It has occurred to me that this pet, partner, incumbent, whatever he is, should have a name, and so I have christened him Steadfast. I call him Steadfast on account of the amazing fortitude displayed the other night when the separate parts of my socket set – including the steel box – rained down on some wood shavings he was arranging. He wasn't happy about it, you could see that, but he stood his ground, heaved himself up on his hindlegs, twitched his whiskers and sniffed indignantly as if to enquire, 'You got any more ironmongery you plan to chuck around?'

He is going to be a good mouse to have in a tight corner.

Apply the Tourniquet Around the Neck

As Medical District Officer for the Exuma Islands, Erwin M Patlak, MD, is at the sharp end of yachting's ill health. The Bahamas, to which his group belong, stand at the gateway to the Caribbean and that makes them a natural funnelling point for the Atlantic's casualties. Add to this the fact that a high proportion of those who come limping in will be first-timers suffering effects of big seas, burning sun and fish that bite – and his experiences become even more untypical. Nonetheless, Dr Patlak's assessment of yachting health makes very disturbing reading.

It was the Victorians, wasn't it, who believed in the healing power of the sea – piers, promenades and that pathetic spectacle, sea cruises for the consumptive. Well, today's yachtsman is worse. He doesn't just perpetuate the myth, he enhances it. One breath of sea air and he is quite prepared to throw all his pills away. As Dr Patlak puts it, 'Why do people with dermatosis, cardio-respiratory disease, gastro-intestinal disturbances, metabolic imbalance, genito-urinary disorders and neoplasma go sailing and leave all their medicines and medical records behind?'

Careless we may be, selfish we are not. There is nobody more willing to extend the balsamic hand than your cruising yachtsman. Not only his medical skill and knowledge but his medications too:

'Practically all the people I see have been treated with borrowed medicine. I have seen steroids used for sore throats, veterinary ointments for ear-aches, fungicides for bacterial infections, and anti-bacterials for fungus.'

'For heaven sake why couldn't you just agree to do the washing up?'

Dr Patlak is harsh, but again he *is* dealing with the extraordinary. DIY surgery, for example. Not something that your average country GP comes across every day. Nor would it help in the general argument to detail those examples of yachtsmen's *makee-mendee* he has chosen – a lady bitten on the breast and a man who partly castrated himself on a windlass.

Something perhaps much easier to understand or agree with are his pronouncements on hygiene, under which title the yachtsman's toilet and laundry habits, food and water, pets and even small children come in for some pretty big stick. Personally, I find his attitude too clinical. As grannie used to say,

'You've got to eat a bit of dirt before you die.' He talks, for example, of our augmenting the ship's unsanitary water supply with rainwater. Rain is a gift from heaven, pure and soft. Ocean sailors become almost reverent about it. 'Gather it by all means', he urges, 'but not in canvas deflectors contaminated in salt and bird droppings.'

For that other kind of drink, he serves the same old kill-joy rhetoric. People on yachts, he observes, drink too much. However, we are spared the usual warning about the liver. The good doctor is more concerned with the immediate effects like drunken cooks attacking their skippers with frying pans, or crews mistaking the number of steps in the companionway.

The sea, he explains, is a nutritious source of protein and vitamins. But, unfortunately, the sea only parts with its gifts grudgingly and he gets one case of ciguatera poisoning a month. He also gets a regular troop of skin divers punctured in various ways. And still to do with extra-yacht activities, injuries caused by water-skis, jet-skis, surf boards and motor-bikes(?).

So there you are. Not, I contest, a proportional view of yachtsmen's health, although it obviously applies to *some* of us. What, then, if you are Caribbean-bound and about to sail into focus? Will you heed the doctor's warning, tow a hospital ship astern, or will you do the other thing and get yourself medically qualified? Not a lot of point, according to our man. 'The greater the professional achievement of doctors and nurses,' he says, 'the worse kind of patients they become.'

And gloomy pessimists too, wouldn't you say, Doctor?

Mrs Bickness of Birkenhead puts copper pennies down the legs of her tights before going afloat to stop her feeling seasick.

"My project's ready for grading, Mr. Big Nose. ...Hey! I'm talkin' to you, squidbrain!"

Swear Box

It will no doubt come as a surprise to learn how hot the Royal Navy used to be on swearing. In fact, every other navy too, since by the 16th century practically every maritime nation had subscribed to the 'Laws of Oleron' which detailed the following punishment:

'If any man defame, vilify or swear at his fellow he shall pay him as many ounces of silver as times he has reviled him.'

This threat, however, did not put an end to the problem, because a century later punishment was stepped up to that of gagging and scraping the offender's tongue. Some pious skippers even ordered a red-hot iron to be placed in the culprit's mouth. A certain Chaplain Teonge wrote in 1675 that he had seen a man secured to the mast for an hour with an iron pin wedged in his mouth simply for *effing* and *blinding*. Then, in the 18th century, a different method was tried when the following article was written into the King's Regulations:

'If any shall be heard to swear, curse or blaspheme the name of God, the Captain is strictly required to punish them for every offence by causing them to wear a wooden collar, or some shameful badge of distinction, for so long time as he shall judge proper.'

Commissioned officers were fined a shilling, and warrant officers sixpence.

American Express

It is not often that the sea delivers its victims but Cyclone Oscar showed this compassion. For 24 hours off Malololailai Island, near Fiji, it hammered American sailor Steve Newman in his 12-metre sloop *Athena*. The yachtsman was near collapse. Then suddenly a huge wave lifted the boat through the surf and landed it on the reception floor of the Plantation Hotel. Mr Newman staggered out on deck. Totally disoriented, he picked up a distress rocket and fired . . . into the ceiling. Next minute the boat was covered in plaster and electrical wiring.

Baltic Charter

'We don't get many *British* charterers coming to Denmark,' said the unhappy-looking man who runs the yacht package holiday. Then, with great deliberation, he laid a strip of cold herring on a square of black bread and popped it into his mouth. 'Perhaps when you go there you will try to see *why*?'

It was the Danish Club restaurant in Knightsbridge. At every table sat homesick Danes munching cold red cabbage and rollmops. Outside, people hurried by in overcoats; above the sky promised snow.

'They don't get many *British* charterers going to Denmark,' I remarked to my wife as she sat up in bed studying the brochure. The cover showed a beach of eye-stretching sand, sparse blades of grass and four people stretched horizontal.

'Well, they *can't* be put off by the crowds,' she observed. 'How far north is it anyway?'

'Oh, on about a level with Dundee.'

'Oyee!' She put the fingers of one hand to her lips, blew on them as if they'd been singed, then waved them in the air. It's a Spanish gesture, and the last sound she was to make concerning our holiday.

The literature said it would be a four-hour drive to the charter base; it took me six. I won't complain; in a normal year I never drive further than Sainsbury's. Danish roads are flat, straight and empty, and with good navigation and a tank full of petrol you never need to make a left turn. (Continental left turns are my *bête noire*; even when I *see* the wire-hung traffic light above the centre of the road and negotiate the oncoming traffic, I still end up in the cycle lane.) It was eight o'clock by the time we arrived, in the pouring rain with the cloud level three feet above our heads and, in the back, two small children each with a cauliflower ear.

A very helpful man came out of the murk, bent his head to the window and emptied the small moat circling the brim of his hat. He dismissed with a smile my concern that he must have been waiting hours, and escorted me down to the boat. A real low profile job.

'You *enjoy* racing?' he enquired as I stepped gingerly along a non-existent side deck clutching a Kermit bag and a teddy bear.

'Well, *yes*, without the family, you know,' I added, hoping he would notice the inference and find us a boat we could stand up in. Suddenly it lurched to one side.

'Ah, here is my *wife*,' I announced and, sensing the menace, retreated for a second load. Let him explain the intricacies of mining beneath the cushions for the toilet and erecting the army bivouac stove. Later, much later, I ventured to ask what she had done with the food.

'He's left some in *there*,' she pointed to a locker. I fumbled inside. 'Black bread and a tin of herrings. Rollmops anybody?'

The next morning, the sun came out and we all felt better. It remained hot and sunny for the next two days and seemed to agree with the Pilot Book which said that Denmark has less rain than the rest of the west European seaboard. My own impression, from the size of the vegetables, confirmed that Denmark did get more sunshine, or else had better fertilizer than mine. Of that other important element, *wind*, there is no shortage. With the highest hill in Denmark still below our office window, the wind flow is steady and uninterrupted.

The waters of Denmark are beautifully protected and, other than those short stretches of coastline exposed to the Baltic's east winds, there is nowhere with a fetch of more than a few miles, consequently no swell worth mentioning. Better than that, there is no tide and no attendant rips or races. In fact, the whole place is about as safe as the Norfolk Broads. Never have I put out of a strange harbour, in a strange boat, with such a feeling of confidence.

Going aground in the middle of an empty sea was

another new experience. I forgot to mention that Danish waters are unusually shallow. The low land had long disappeared, a mist had settled, there wasn't a sail or mast to be seen and my little girl, I noticed, was praying very hard in the cabin. Did I also omit to tell you that thanks to an absolute plethora of marinas in these parts nobody ever tows, or perhaps even *owns*, a dinghy. Kedging was therefore out of the question, even supposing we found the deep water which, according to the chart, was 10 miles to the north. The only thing to do was to heel the boat by shifting weights, sheeting in hard and driving off under engine – a classic manoeuvre at home, but interpreted by people here perhaps as a boat with an enviable wind? After repeated attempts, God finally got us off – at least that is what my daughter said and I'm not the one to disagree.

Normally shallow water presents no problem because channels are clearly marked and local charts are simple to follow. There are plenty of foreign yachts plying the coastal routes and hopping from island to island. We *hopped* to an island to sit out our second depression. A typical disaster. Denmark . . . notorious night-life . . . world-famous lager . . . a beautiful archipelago of 406 islands and I had to pick a vice*less*, pub*less* nature reserve. The handbook described the village as 'time preserved'. I think mummified might have been more apt. A collection of dark little cottages, a church, a shop charging more than Oxford Street, and every inhabitant down in his cellar, head in a bucket of *schnapps*. Certainly nobody came out in the rain – except the *fool Anglais* of course. I frog-marched my family five times around the island until our wardrobe of dry clothes finally ran out and it was back to the boat for another exciting round of 'I-spy'.

The next day I discovered that it wasn't poor

Home is the Sailor

navigation that had put us aground, but a 15 degree error in the compass. Aren't yacht harbours marvellous for checking your compass? First look on the harbour chart and then, to make sure, compare your compass with your neighbour's.

'Excuse me, do you speak English?'

'A liddle.'

'Would you mind telling me *what* your boat is steering?'

End of conversation.

In Denmark yacht harbours proliferate. With tideless waters and ten-inch seas, they must be dirt cheap to build. Food is expensive, but then that is the beauty of being able to take the car and freighting your own provisions. It leaves a little extra cash to spend on the local specialities. My favourite was *Sodmalk*. The first time I met *Sodmalk* it was floating in my tea, in lumps.

'Look!' I explained to the little old lady who owned the shop. 'I think this milk is *off*!' I screwed up my nose and clasped my throat to make sure the message went home. She gave me a smile of understanding and exchanged my broached cartoon with a fresh one. Twenty minutes later I was back, with the same complaint and into my throat clutching routine. Once again *Sodmalks* were exchanged, smiles and courtesies too, although I thought I heard her bolt the door.

'Perhaps,' suggested my wife, 'if you poured it over your cornflakes instead of in your tea you might enjoy it.' She was right; it turned out to be a sort of sour cream and over cereals absolutely delicious. Sodmalk: you'll remember the name.

For courtesy and quiet helpfulness, the Danes can have few equals. The lady in the shop; the super couple who, seeing we were fed up in the rain, invited us home to dinner; and the man who owned the charter boat, far too polite to come aboard to check if anything was lost or broken. But

68

it was my son who had the final taste of Danish hospitality when he got lost on a walkabout coming home on the ferry. *'William from England is looking for his Mummy,'* the loudspeaker boomed and two guilty parents hurried out of the Duty Free shop. At the information desk a long queue stood ignored and unattended while two beautiful girls in crisp white blouses soaked in tears were attempting to console him.

Ah! that I was $4\frac{1}{2}$ again.

Foaming Along

A West Country cure for leaking seams is yellow soap which first softens and then *in salt water* congeals, taking on the consistency of processed Cheddar cheese.

The Cornish luggers used to be planked in softwood on oak; no caulking, but yellow soap rubbed into all the seams. Then launched off and allowed to sink for a few tides until they had taken up.

A yachtsman bought a Cornish fishing boat before the war to convert into a yacht. He noticed several bars of yellow soap in the after locker, but merely thought how clean the former crew must have been. He sailed her up Channel and into the Thames without incident; but when he reached Teddington and locked into fresh water, she produced a beautiful lather, then sank.

A lady neighbour of genteel disposition asked my Spanish wife if she preferred going to the swimming pool or sea bathing?

'I'm frightened to swim in the sea,' said my wife, 'in case I step on a *crap.*'

Cockroaches once became such a menace to ships in the Japanese Navy that every sailor who managed to catch and bottle 300 cockroaches was given a day's leave. It was actually called 'Cockroach leave' – however you say that in Japanese.

A dinghy manufacturer placed an advertisement in a boat market magazine. A few days later they phoned him.

'Just checking your boat's construction,' the girl said, '*Iroko*. What's that – some kind of glassfibre?'

Ever wondered why blue is the popular colour for seafarers? It dates from the time of the Romans. They were fond of leading their attacks with a particularly fast vessel called a *Pictae*, and to help these ships go undetected by the enemy, the hulls, sails and the crew's uniforms were all dyed blue.

Sick Joke

'*Great amusement is afforded by the gannet snare*' wrote one eminent Victorian yachtsman. After some researches I eventually found out what this was.

'It's alright sweetheart, Daddy said he will drive home and get Teddy's life-jacket.'

The gannet snare is a heavy plank of wood painted green and floating on the sea with a piece of fish offal nailed to it. The gannet, who is hungry, short-sighted, or perhaps both, sees the plank of wood (or rather he doesn't) and proceeds to dive on the offal from a great height. By the time he sees the joke it's too late and, unable to pull out of the dive, he woodpeckers on the hatchboard.

Sick Sailors

The Romans' answer to seasickness was a thin strip of copper stuck to the inside of each foot. Placed at the outset of the voyage, it was believed that bad humours caused by the malady would drain and be drawn out of the body through the balls of the feet. If it was working properly, the copper then turned green.

Some Victorians believed that three sheets of blotting paper worn inside the vest were an infallible preventive to seasickness. Others fancied that a little sugar dipped in creosote was more efficacious.

The Spanish conquistadors' answer to the problem was celibacy – and chicken broth.

Davy Jones Gets a Shake Up

The bottom of the sea. How do you imagine it? As peaceful as a grave, dark and still where little ever moves save for a lazy crustacean opening an eye, or an upward spiralling weed.

Where do these impressions come from? Jules Verne, Cousteau's cameras? The latest information is that it's entirely fictitious – they have storms down there the like of which we have never seen. More powerful than any hurricane and more damaging than an H-bomb, they tear off mighty crags of rock and stir up huge clouds of sediment. And yet not a whisper of it ever comes up to the surface. Oceanologists using readings taken from sonar buoys and laser beams have discovered there is a steady 5km/hr current of cold water moving over the ocean floor. Predominantly, this is water melting from the Poles. But there are equally fast moving belts of warmer, salty water which generate from the equatorial regions. Over smooth ground the two currents meet harmoniously; like air masses, the colder current drives a shallow wedge under the warm current. However, it's over rough ground that the trouble starts – when two opposing currents, each with hundreds of cubic miles of water, collide head on over rocks. That is when these tremendous disturbances occur.

But storms in the deep are not the only new-found phenomenon. Scientists have also discovered that the sea is not level as we imagine it to be but consists of a number of hills, valleys and slopes. Before the US SEASAT satellite fizzled out in the late 1970s, it sent back to earth some 50 million altimeter readings, each accurate to a quarter of an inch. These have since been compiled and one remarkable fact has emerged, that the Mediterranean between Cannes and Algiers slopes down 25 feet.

Smooth Work

Method for achieving a really smooth bottom described by a well-heeled Victorian yachtsman:

'I would first set half a dozen cabinet makers to work to plane, scrape and sandpaper the bottom. After this I would bring on the caulkers to attend the seams. After the caulkers are done I would send for the cabinet makers once against to plane, scrape and sandpaper the surplus. Six well-recommended coach painters are then employed to apply three coats of primer, a coat of putty, a rub down with pumice stone, more primer, a couple of coats of white lead and a finishing coat of copal varnish. Some workers may think this preparation unnecessary, but their objections must be dismissed for it is only by stepping boldly out of the old

'All that money having the bottom scrubbed and we're still at the back of the fleet.'

routine system that we can ever expect to attain perfection.'

It's the *we* bit that gets you.

The Polyestermite

'I think you may be interested in my discovery.' That was as much as the Lloyds surveyor would say on the telephone. Hardly the sort of invitation to lure one down to the coast on a wintry afternoon – except for the note of urgency in his voice.

We had arranged to meet near the boat hoist but he was already by the gate when I arrived, a jam-jar in his hand. 'Look at *this*.' He thrust his arm through the car window. The jam-jar held a small prawn-like creature.

'What is it?' I asked, mistrustful of seafood.

'It's a *polyestermite*. The first one we've managed to catch.'

I looked dumb. 'A polyestermite?' I asked.

'Yes, haven't you *heard*, they eat glassfibre boats.'

He led me across to a boat which was lying in her cradle. 'This is where we found the little horror,' he explained and banged the hull with his hammer. A shower of white powder fell to the ground.

'You mean to say they've done *this*!' The hull looked like a section drawing through an ant colony.

'Yes,' he replied. 'In three days. She was as sound as a bell when the owner left her on Sunday. Come Friday he'll be able to sweep her away with a broom.'

I dusted my shoulders and sat down to listen while he told me the whole incredible story. It appears that, with the demise of wooden boats, the common gribble or shipworm began to go hungry. There was a great migration to wooden piers, wharves and things like that, but soon these were all

'C'mon, say hello to the clever surveyor.'

eaten up and starvation followed. Eventually and inevitably there was cannibalism, a situation in which only the toughest of the species survived. Not only that but the creatures actually grew stronger and larger due to the hormone rich diet their mates had provided; they became super-gribble.

Opinions are divided as to the precise stage when the super-gribble evolved into the polyestermite but it was in a relatively short period of time. Nature adapted itself to man's preference for glassfibre and gave this new species the facility with which to eat it. In chemical terms this was a masticatory-assisted gland containing a powerful solvent acid. The acid, which chemists have found to be a hundred times stronger than nail varnish remover, is excreted onto the gel coat and then dispersed by the insect's feet – some of the forelegs are shaped like glue spreaders for the purpose. The acid dissolves the gel coat and the creature is quickly through to the chopped strand mat, or woven rovings. It is a prolific eater and can, during a feeding frenzy or during mating, when it needs a lot of energy, eat fourteen times its own weight. The polyestermite (*resinus pestus domestos*) was first discovered in America where it was found eating plastic detergent bottles on the Hudson River, a splendid debut which instantly endeared it to the Friends of the Earth. Indeed it was a rapturous beginning, and a Wisconsin candidate, running for Congress on a conservation ticket, even adopted the polyestermite as his motif. But then somebody found them quietly chewing away on the recently laid Alaskan pipeline, and the honeymoon promptly ended.

Despite strict surveillance at the ports and a ban imposed by the Ministry of Agriculture and Fisheries, *resinus pestus domestos* came to Britain some time last winter. Already it is firmly established along the south coast, where its notoriety has even overshadowed the fast-growing Japanese seaweed. So far no effective antidote has been found, although everything including banned insecticides has been tried – it actually *enjoys* some of the better known proprietary brands.

Now, there is one more alarming fact which has just been discovered. Government scientists working at the Germ Warfare Establishment at Porton Down near Salisbury have found that the polyestermite is biologically *double-ended*. That is to say, it has a mouth at each end; so, with mandibles at the front and nippers at the rear, it can lie on its back in a marina and eat two boats at once.

I asked the Lloyds surveyor if there was anything, just anything, which owners could do to protect their boats from the ravages of this pest. There was only one sure remedy, he said, expensive but totally effective.

'And what is that?'

'Sheathe the boat in wood.'

(The polyestermite was first released on the boating public at the 1970 Boat Show. By summer, *resinus pestus domestos* was responsible for new harbour buoys disappearing in Durban, for ruining one country's Admiral's Cup chances and even disrupting the oil flow in Abadan.)

Falling Standards

Sir Hugo de Bathe, fine handle that he had, is still better remembered as the second Mr Lillie Langtry. Nonetheless, in his own right the man had style. Once, on a cruise from New York, he fell overboard and the yacht's gig was lowered to go to his rescue. He was treading water when they reached him, quite composed. He had his yachting hat on his head and his monocle fixed in place. He was, however, in a very bad humour.

'Who the *hell* do you think I am?' was his greeting to the rescuers.

'Why, you are the owner, Sir Hugo, sir,' replied the seamen in some surprise.

'That being the case, you can God-damned well return and fetch out the long boat. And have the captain in command, you hear? And while you're at it, get into your dress blues and show some spit and polish. We'll have style around here when the owner falls overboard.'

Bird Dropping Boat

A British ship foundered in the South Atlantic in the early 19th century and one of its lifeboats eventually fetched up on a rocky deserted island. For the half-dozen survivors, the situation looked hopeless; there was no food other than a few berries and scarcely any shelter or protection from the Antarctic winter which was quickly setting in. Rescue was out of the question; few if any ships came this far south and their own boat had been damaged beyond repair.

It was then that the mate, who was in charge of

Robot Goes to Sea

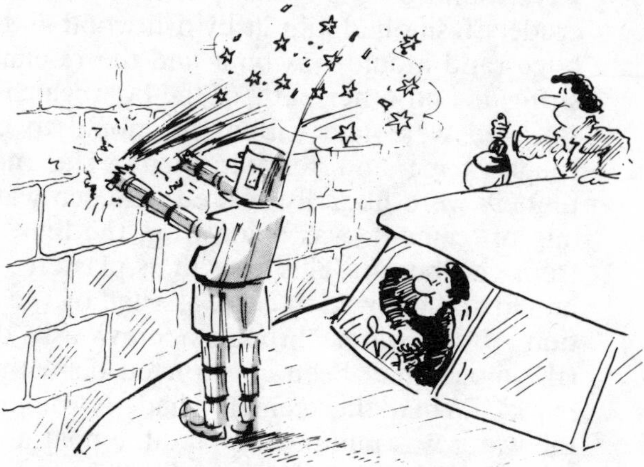

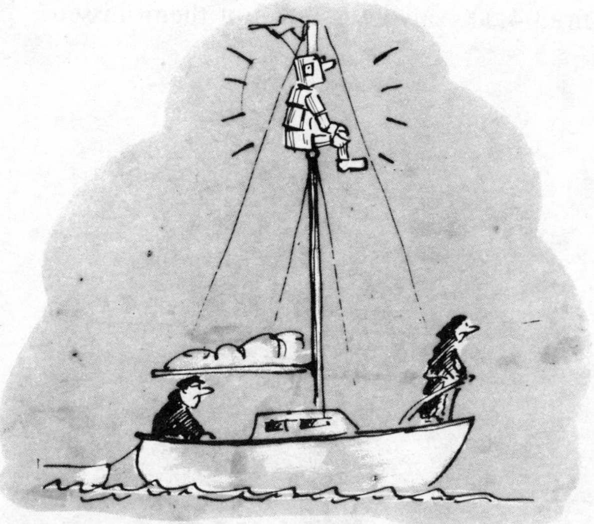

the party, hit on a desperate idea. He had the men collect some of the huge deposits of birdlime that were found on the rocks overhead and fired it in a crudely fashioned kiln lit by driftwood and twigs. A huge sand mould was built and the remaining ribs, stringers and other parts of the boat which could be salvaged were laid within the mould to provide a rough shape and reinforcement. The mould and timbers were liberally soaked with sea water and a mix of 'cement' was made from the lime and sand from the beach. This was then plastered into the mould and allowed to cure, assisted by the introduction of sea water through a previously dug canal (the mould had been constructed beneath the HW mark). When the 'cement' had thoroughly cured, the water was pumped out and the boat made ready for sea. With the blessing of good weather, these innovative men later arrived in South America in the world's first concrete boat!

At the Battle of Jutland, the British Grand Fleet fired 4,000 salvoes – 3,860 of them missed.

The female cockroach is correctly called a *nymph* and the male is a *lobster*. And the biologist who thought those delights up obviously has never had one turn around and spit in his eye like one did to me when I went to clear it off the messroom table.

When the gallery of the first Eddystone Lighthouse went up in flames, the 90-year-old keeper rushed out the door, looked up and gasped in horror just as a piece of molten lead was coming down. He swallowed it. He survived, but the problem was trying to convince his doctor it had really happened. It was not until after his death that the piece of lead was recovered. Today it can be found in the British Medical Museum.

England Expects – Despite the Cuts

HMS Incredible lay on her trailer in a corner of Shoreham's esplanade car park. The rain was falling heavily as two oilskinned figures drew close.

'Is that her?' asked one. The other nodded. 'Right, here we go then,' and between them they trundled Britain's latest warship between the rows of cars toward the public slip. A group of shift-workers returning home stopped and gave a small cheer. 'Poor devils,' said a man and threw his newspaper into the harbour. It drifted down on *Incredible*. NO FISH WAR THIS YEAR the headline read. The skies grew more leaden; the rain continued to beat down.

Down below, Lt Cmdr 'Tiger' Davenport stirred uneasily; there was somebody in his cabin. A slow rhythmic breathing, a smell of stale liquor – wherever was it coming from? He turned his head and saw a shape in the opposite bunk. Covered in a blanket, it was slowly rising and falling. He snatched the blanket back. A heavy-jowled man in a vest sat up.

'Who the hell are you?'

'9635421 Harris G,' came the slow but automatic reply. The figure glanced about him, blinking his eyes and enquiring, 'Ere – where's this then? I faught vis was the stoker's mess!'

'*That* half, yes,' replied his commanding officer, pushing the sailor to the far side of the vee berth. 'This half happens to be the wardroom.'

'Oh well,' said Harris, 'if I'm in me rightful place you won't mind if I smokes then.' He offered Davenport a Woodbine. Just then the two men heard the sound of a diesel engine and the dark shadow of the picket boat manoeuvring alongside. 'Permission to come aboard, Sir.'

'Oh, that'll be the new Number One,' announced Davenport, jumping up and pulling on his trousers. 'Right ho, Number One, carry on.' The invitation was followed by a tremendous crash above Harris's head. The boat heeled violently; his wristwatch, cigarette lighter and small change rained down from the shelf. Seconds later a partly-trousered commanding officer landed on top of him.

'My golly, these boats are a bit tippy,' chirped the new arrival. 'ARE YOU THERE, SKIPPER?'

'No need to *shout*, Number One,' said Davenport, sidling alongside him under the hatch, where he was at last able to pull up his trousers. 'We're only twelve foot long, y'know!'

'Sorry, sir. Look, I've brought you the signals.' Davenport took the brown envelope and tore open the reusable label.

'Damn,' he said as he read the message. 'It's the East Coast for us again.'

'B . . . b . . . but I thought that was B flotilla's patch,' stammered the First Lieutenant.

'They're gone,' replied Davenport laconically.

'You mean . . .'

'That's right, bloody Admiralty's fallen behind with the payments again. The bailiff has impounded them in Harwich.' He looked around. 'HARRIS!' he called. A sullen face popped up from the forehatch. 'Ah! Harris, better get your engine ready, we're leaving for the East Coast.'

The stoker gripped the coaming. 'The *where*?' he asked incredulously, his lower lip beginning to tremble.

'Oh, don't worry, Harris,' soothed the young

commander. 'We're not sailing there. They've booked us with Sealink.'

At 0600 the next day a car ferry stopped in the grey-green waters of the Thames Estuary and those passengers foolish enough to be on deck at that hour saw the bow doors open and the little grey warship lowered into the sea. They would also have seen, had they lifted their sleepy eyes, a small speck on the horizon.

'Right, after the bastards!' roared Lt Cmdr Davenport. Harris allowed himself a last sardonic grin and, gripping the cord with an oily rag, gunned the Seagull outboard into life. Within seconds they were lost in spray.

On the bridge of the French mussel dredger *La Gaie Fishmongère*, holds crammed with illicitly caught British kippers, the skipper handed his engineer a pair of glasses.

'Zose crazy rosbifs,' he breathed admiringly, 'fancy waterskiing in weazzer like zis.' The engineer watched in disbelief as *Incredible* shot out from under the bow. He saw the white flag with the red cross tied to a boathook and heard the Britisher's words through a megaphone.

'STOORP CARRYWING OUT YOUR HIN-TENSHUNS!'

Understanding was lost in the wind. 'Ees no *waterskiing*,' the engineer announced, 'ees the Missions to Seamen come to change our library books! Quick, give zem a lee.'

Aboard *Incredible* the well-intentioned man-oeuvre was misunderstood. 'The Frogs are trying to *escape*!' screamed the First Lieutenant.

'*Are* they, by God!' yelled Davenport. 'We'll see about that!' He spun the wheel and drove the little ship across the Frenchman's bow. It was a desperate but vain attempt, for at that precise moment a huge wave picked *Incredible* up and spun her into the air.

'What's 'appened?' demanded the stunned

French skipper of a now doomed vessel. From the engine room sounds of winging nuts and bolts could be heard and the steam pressure dropped to zero.

' 'Ow do I know what's 'appened,' shrugged the engineer, hurrying out of the wheelhouse. 'Ees not everyday a leetel boat comes down zer funnel.'

'And don't drink any.'

If It Squeaks . . .

My *Seaman's Practical Pocket Book* has some 'useful tips'. Here is a selection.

Squeaky boots Can be cured by driving a little wooden dowel through the sole or soaking in linseed oil.

To frost a window Mix half a cupful of beer with 2 oz of Epsom Salts.

Rats To rid the vessel of rats, set traps, kill the females and let the males go free. They will soon resort to cannibalism(?).

Fire extinguisher A cheap fire extinguisher can be made by dissolving a little Pearlash in water.

Notices to Mariners
(Facts behind the news)

EAST AFRICA – Mozambique Channel – Beacons non-existent

CHILE – Iquique – Coastal radio station discontinued

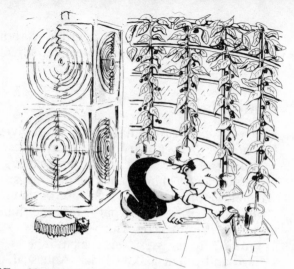

GREECE – Nisis Kithnos Lighthouse – Range reduced

PACIFIC OCEAN – Palmerston Island – Amendment lies 3 miles south-east

SUMATRA – Aroih Raya – Dangerous shoal reported

Pearlash, it explains, is a crude carbonate of potash which has an almost immediate effect on the fire. I expect the water helps.

Foul Plague

Feel your expensive anti-fouling is not giving value for money? Why not try these alternatives:

From the West Country, a fisherman's mix of creosote, Jeyes Fluid and seagull eggs. Or for warmer waters the stuff Arabs use on their dhows? A mixture of melted goat's fat and lime – it's important to put it on with your fingers.

Finally, from Essex, this recipe;

Two and a half gallons black Aquaseal,

1 pint copper sulphate,

2 pints weed killer,

$\frac{1}{2}$ pint ant and insect killer,

2 sachets of Rentokill rat poison.

'Anti-foulin', no sir. We jist leaves the big staysail up till the last minute and her bottom shines up on the pebbles a treat.'

This all works out at about £10 per three-gallon mix, and is claimed by its creator to give excellent results.

Rub-a-Dub-Dub

. . . Three men in a tub were rescued six miles out in the Wash after a 24-hour search. The survivors explained they had gone to sea in a bathtub to raise money for charity. The men were an engineer, a publican and a gardener. The butcher, the baker and the candlestick maker stayed home.

It's an Investment

I was watching some old TV news-reels the other night about putting a man on the moon. The presenter was saying how expensive it had been – billions and billions of dollars. Then as the two astronauts began to hunt around in the dust for the ship's ignition key, the thought occurred to me that mile for mile I bet space travel is no more expensive than sailing. What is it to the moon? About 250,000 miles they reckon. I haven't even got as far as the Isle of Wight but I've blown every penny of our savings.

Lately, bills have been raining down on me like hailstones; I've got them spiked here by the chair. There's the mooring chain and sinkers, the insurance, the crane hire charge and the quote for the launching. And all these things are extras of course, after the boat has been paid for. However can a man like me afford a sport that exclusively belongs to Greek shipping millionaires and princes?

Just then my wife appeared at the door, wiped the hair from her eyes and said, 'Well, that's the O'Reillys' and Jenkins' washing finished, only Sam's Diner left to do.'

'Come and sit down and rest your bones,' I invited, and patted the cushion next to me. In a while, she was sleeping peacefully, little beads of perspiration bubbling across her forehead and matting her hair. I looked at her hands bleached white and wrinkled and in that moment of compassion whispered in her ear, 'No more scrubbing down by the river for you, My Sweet, I'm gonna buy you a washing machine.' She awoke with a start. Her hand reached involuntarily for mine.

'But darling,' she protested, 'you've *still* got your satellite navigation system to pay for.'

'True,' I said and fell back, beaten by the power of her argument. I went down to the club after that and, sitting at the bar, heard a familiar voice below me.

'Shoeshine, mister?'

'Good heavens! It's Hawkesworth Junior, isn't it? Doesn't your papa run a Speedbird 15?'

'Gotta Moonraker Eclipse now,' the urchin replied brightly. 'Keeps it down at Bay View Marina.'

Any doubts or misgivings I might have had about the exploitation of children vanished in an instant. I have never seen a boy show such pride. And what self-confidence! The panache with which he wiped his nose on his sleeve had to be seen to be believed; the arrogant way he bit into a dry crust of bread kept in his pocket; traits such as these seldom are seen in the children of indulgent parents.

Morning brought the usual rain of final demands, solicitors' threats and a man to turn off the electricity. 'God, is there no end to these predators?' I wondered and a hunger-crazed Labrador sank his fangs in my leg. I thought this was supposed to be the age of leisure. Well, why can't they let a man enjoy his simple pleasures – the wind, the sea, the sky and the sun . . . And a boat that costs £22,000 just to enjoy 'em from.

'We got a council grant for the bathroom.'

'Oh *nuts*,' I said, 'I can't sit around here all day. I'm going to buy the roller-furling gear for the staysail.'

'You're not taking *that* money,' she protested as I stuck my hand inside the old teapot. 'That's my potato-digging money. I was saving it to buy the children some shoes.'

'Shoes! *Shoes*!' I exploded. 'Good God, woman, summer's coming.' I admit that sometimes this indulgence does bother me, especially at night. I lie awake and listen to the wind peeling off the roof tiles and billowing the wallpaper in the kids' room and I think to myself that maybe it is true what they say about sailing people being selfish. I took my problem to a wise old man who lives near. Did he think I was justified to spend so much money on the boat and cause my family so much deprivation?

'Son,' he said, 'it's an investment in happiness and health. At least you have something to show. What about these husbands and fathers who fritter away their money on horses, tobacco and drink?'

A great comfort, that old man. I went in with one problem on my mind and came out with three more.

The Paint Job

'Wants to know if we can spare him half a pint of thinner.'

'Alf . . . here a minute, something's grabbed
hold of me scraper.'

'Really, Hoskins, they look terribly faded.
Can't we freshen them up?'

Under Starter's Orders

It's not beyond the realms of possibility that we shall one day see a fish race. We have, after all, managed to engender a competitive spirit into a number of our fellow species, greyhounds, horses, pigeons, cockroaches . . .

One can see some organising difficulties; the fact that you'd have predator and prey all running in the same race would make betting difficult. Then again, a fish Derby or Ascot would never excite the same sartorial interest.

The start would be the most exciting part. Probably you have noticed with your own goldfish bowl, how remarkably fast the fish react when you switch on the light and they see the magnified face of the cat. Well, it's reckoned that fish, from a standing start, can be at their top speed in less than a twentieth of a second. Deceleration is just as fast; but then it would have to be, living in a goldfish bowl.

The finish is a foregone conclusion. The swordfish would be the winner; he is thought to be the fastest fish in the sea. He hasn't actually been 'clocked', but one ran his sword into the side of a wooden ship and, working it back – he was in about 13 inches – they estimated that he must have been doing between 80 and 100 knots on impact.

Lane spacing could be difficult with entries like the 120-ton blue whale to consider. He, incidentally, can cruise at 14 knots. Top speed is thought to be around 20 knots but only in short bursts, like when he's harpooned. But then most cetacea are reasonably fast; the dolphin still seems able to outpace many of the world's fastest ships, while even the grampus (whatever that is?) can do 18 knots.

Having what most designers concede to be the most perfect streamlined shape possible the blue tunny should do well on handicap – one towed an angler and his boat 120 miles out to sea, apparently.

Surprisingly, the little mackerel can swim faster than the tunny and, since he is the latter's prime diet, frequently has to. One fish that *has* been accurately 'clocked' is the bonefish. He once reeled off 400 feet of line in 20.4 seconds which works out at about 40 mph.

If the stewards allow leaping and flying, then the salmon and flying fish would be able to enter. The salmon can do roughly 18 knots, flying fish leave the water at between 15 and 20 knots and can reach up to 55 knots during flight.

Even if they could handle the salt water, it is doubtful if many fresh-water fish would enter. They are abysmally slow: 10 knots for the trout, 4 knots for the roach. In racing terms, simply non-starters.

'Now the bunny goes behind the tree and back down his hole.'

Swallows and Amazons for What?

Where did Arthur Ransome find such marvellous children for his crews; and why do WE always get the other sort?

'Listen children, I have a wonderful surprise. You know that old dinghy in the boathouse, the *Swallow*. Well, I have repaired her! So tomorrow you could take her and explore that island in the lake, now isn't that exciting!' Their father paused and searched the three blank faces. 'Just think, a voyage of discovery in the good ship *Swallow*. John can be captain, Susan . . . Susan, please pay attention, you can see to your eye-liner later, you can be mate and cook. Roger! You're the youngest so you'll have to be ship's boy – and lookout of course, very important. And Titty . . . Where's Titty, children?'

'Oh, she's all screwed up again.'

'Pardon?'

'She's in a sulk up in her room,' said Roger.

'Well, she can be *Able Seaman* Titty.'

'Dad.'

'Yes, John.'

'Dad, do you have to carry on like this, it's so embarrassing. . . .'

Their father looked crestfallen. 'Well, I thought you'd like to sail to the island and camp, and light a fire, and cook your own meals, and go exploring . . .'

'Yeah, okay, Dad, but do we have to have this *Captain, Mate, Able Seaman*, business?'

'Yes, and why pick me as the cook?' moaned Susan. 'That's sexist.'

A sound of sobbing silenced all further complaint. Sobbing punctuated by broken utterances and gasps. It was Roger. His father asked for a translation. 'He says he doesn't want to be Ship's Boy,' explained his sister. 'He wants to be Hannibal

Smith from the *A-Team*.'

The parents were up early the next morning to prepare things. Mother got the food ready and put it into labelled containers. She also made sure there was plenty of warm clothing and the children had their boots. Father sorted out the camping equipment and then went down to the *Swallow* to set up the mast and sail. When all had been finally made ready and the last detail checked, the children got out of bed.

Roger was the first one down, he was always a speedy dresser; an edge he managed to maintain on his brother and sisters by the simple expedient of wearing his clothes to bed.

'We have decided that you can sail in the *Swallow* and Daddy will escort you in the Dory,' said Mother when the children had assembled for breakfast.

'*That's* not fair!' they chorused. 'He's the one who's always raving about sailing, let him take the dinghy and we'll have the Dory.'

Roger added his point. 'We'll need a fast boat in case we get attacked by perverts.'

'The word is *pirates*,' corrected his mother.

'You don't get pirates in the Lake District, stupid,' said Susan. John said that if his sister was going to be cook the biggest danger they would face would be salmonella poisoning.

By ten o'clock the children were ready to leave. Titty had been prised moodily out of bed and together they trudged down to the *Swallow*. Their father had taught them to sail years before and although competent, they were unenthusiastic. Slowly they went through the motions of hoisting sail, shipping the rudder and letting go the ropes and finally, with tracks from *The Slade*'s latest album echoing across the lake, they were gone.

It was a long day for the parents. They had arranged that Father would visit at 4 o'clock, just to

see if there was anything they needed. Mother had checked Susan had her mirror and frequently looked out of her kitchen window for a flash from this improvised heliograph. In the garden, Father was just as anxious and, like his wife, looked continually in the direction of the island. He was looking for smoke, but not a signal, just an uneasy feeling he had that they would set the place alight.

The concern was all quite unnecessary for when 4 o'clock came and their father arrived on the island he found things extremely well organised. They had cleared a space for an open-air disco and barbecue, while down on the beach Roger had built a Foreign Legion fort with underground garage. Even Titty, with her thumb in her mouth, had been busy and arranged an ornamental shell garden.

'Well, this is fine,' said their father when the tour had been finished. 'I'm glad to see you making such a *comfortable* camp. But isn't it time you thought about putting up the tent?'

'Waffor?'

'John, please don't talk like that. To spend the night here, of course, that's what for.'

'*Huh!* Catch me sleeping out here,' said his son, 'when I got a perfectly good bed over there!' He nodded towards the house.

'Me too,' added Susan. Then looking up at her father with an old-fashioned look, she went on, 'I *am* twelve, you know Daddy; I've gone through the Brown Owl and Arkala bit.'

'If we hurry,' put in Roger, 'I'll just be in time to watch *Fall Guy*.'

It was so peaceful on the island once the children had gone. Their father popped the last sausage into his mouth and leaned back in deep contentment. The moon had thrown the shadow of a branch over the roof of the tent. He studied it for a while. Reflections, he thought, a good time for reflections. These children of his, where had they gone wrong? Was it outside influences, the school, the television? Or had their mother pampered them too much.

Titty, for example. Why was she so withdrawn? He stopped suddenly. Something was digging into his back. He grabbed the torch and pulled back the groundsheet to find he had camped on top of the ornamental garden. And something else he hadn't noticed – a skull and crossbones and the words 'I'LL GET THEM FOR CALLING ME TITTY'.

Dutch Spook Keeps Low Profile

It's forty years now since the *Flying Dutchman* has been seen, and little wonder the legend is dying. Gone are the days when he held supernatural star billing. His place is long taken by more approachable apparitions for he always was a remote and rather aloof ghost consumed with his own sense of purpose. Also, there was that curse that all who saw him died soon afterwards.

In 1680, according to port records in Amsterdam, one Captain Vanderdecken sailed bound for Batavia. His ship hit endless storms off the Cape of Good Hope and for weeks battled on with her rudder damaged and most of her canvas shredded. Vanderdecken refused to be beaten and it was from this blind obstinacy that the legend began. He defied the Almighty to stop him from rounding the Cape 'though I should cruise to Judgement Day'. God took up the challenge and the Dutchman has been battling since.

There have been a number of sightings. In 1823 the captain of HMS *Leven* reportedly saw the ghost ship through his glasses. Later, in 1879, the officers, passengers and crew of the steamer *Pretoria* saw an old fashioned sailing ship burning blue distress lights but when the steamer turned to render assistance the sailing ship had gone. But the most notable sighting of all is that claimed by no less a royal personage than King George V while serving as a midshipman in HMS *Bacchante*. This was in

1881 and the young prince, as he was then, described the event in his diary:

'The look-out man on the forecastle reported her as close to the port bow, where also the officer of the watch clearly saw her . . . A strange red light as of a phantom ship all aglow, in the midst of which light the mast, spars and sails of a brig two hundred yards distant stood out in strong relief as she came up.'

Two other navy ships which were in company also saw a strange red light as the *Flying Dutchman* crossed *Bacchante*'s bows. Then, just as the legend prophesied, a tragedy struck when, 12 hours later, the seaman who had been lookout fell to his death.

The last sighting was just before the last war when people on the beach at False Bay saw a sailing ship with all sails set and drawing. The puzzling thing was that there was no wind at the time and a mist hung over the Bay. Then, just as it seemed she would run ashore, she suddenly vanished and no one has seen her since.

Red Sails in the Sunset

What success do the Russians hope to achieve with their latest incursion into the West – the Cruise Liner? Will they be able to equal the quality of decadence we are used to?

Captain Ivan Ivanovitch stood on the bridge of his ship in Southampton docks taking photographs of a passing frigate. He was pleased with himself, his masters would be pleased. Now what had he done with his copy of *Jane's Fighting Ships*? Damn fine book for a woman.

'Captain Ivan Ivanovitch,' a voice spoke suddenly in his ear.

He started. 'Oh, it's you, Alexis Alexikoff. Why do you have to creep up on me like that?' Alexis Alexikoff was always creeping up on people. He

had been trained to. A former military attaché in Washington and familiar figure on the cocktail circuit, the suddenness of his approach was intended to surprise information out of people. In fact all it had achieved was a great number of spilled drinks and he had been finally called home in disgrace. Although professionally suited to the role of ship's entertainments officer through his exposure to Western society, he was completely unsuited in temperament. He had a solemn face and was given to uncontrollable bouts of tears.

'Well, Alexis Alexikoff, have you found interesting passengers for the Captain's table: research chemists, micro-chip technicians and metallurgists? I particularly need metallurgists . . .'

But before he could reply a toot from the tug's whistle indicated that the ship was ready to sail, a reminder also voiced by a crowd on the quay, who sent up a cheer and a barrage of toilet rolls. One roll landed complete at the captain's feet. He immediately grabbed it and stuffed it in his pocket. Olga would be pleased, she was tired of tearing up squares of *Izvestia*.

*'One thing we've learnt on this cruise.
We've nothing to fear from the Russians.'*

Down below, in the public room named and
commemorated after the Battle of Stalingrad with a
mural of 56,000 Wehrmacht prisoners marching
around the room, Joe and Mavis Jolliffe sat
enjoying a bowl of soup. 'It's ever so nice of the
captain 'aving us sit at his table tonight, Joe,' said
Mavis. But Joe Jolliffe, who dealt in scrap metals,
wasn't listening. He was troubled; a big man in a
homburg and a double-breasted suit kept watching
him.

'Good evening, Comrades,' said the Captain
jauntily as he took his seat at the table for dinner. 'I
am late, so sorry. The stupid pilot wanted to go out
through the Needles Channel ven he *knows* I always
look in at Portsmouth. But now ve drink, yes?' And

103

with that he leapt to his feet and went around the table emptying his guests' tumblers of water and refilling them with vodka which he dispensed from a large demijohn. 'In Russia ve drink so!' Upon which he leaned back, emptied the vodka down his throat and sent the empty tumbler spinning towards the mock fireplace. A balalaika struck up and, at a signal from the captain, six commis waiters came handspringing across the tables. Soon the entire dining saloon was filled with the sound of tinkling glass, fevered handclaps and Cossack war cries. Contrived it may have been, but Joe had to admit its infectiousness and by ten o'clock he found himself under the table screened on four sides by a tablecloth slurring out the secrets of his scrap metal business to a man in a double-breasted suit.

'I can't pick up Terry Wogan on this,' said Mavis Jolliffe the next morning as she twiddled the radio in their cabin. Her husband raised a spinning head from his pillow.

'I should have thought that wiv all them aerials they got you could have picked up the Flying Doctor.' At that moment martial music flooded into the room. 'There you are,' said Joe. 'You've got something now.'

'That's not on the radio, Joe,' his wife pointed out, 'that's upstairs. Come on, we'll go up and see.'

The entire games deck had been cleared and strung with banners. On top of the radio shack which overlooked the deck a rostrum had been created. They could see a row of frozen faces, some in fur caps, some in black homburgs, some in uniform caps with medals. As the couple turned they saw the procession start up. From the starboard side of the boat deck they came, the entire ship's crew, cooks, stewards, hairdressers, masseurs, all goosestepping to the sound of the ship's band. They were led by the Master-at-Arms, with automatic weapons; then came the mechanised section, 200 serving trolleys in lines of six with silver plate all sparkling; next the butchers, each one parading a side of beef; then button boys, lift attendants, laundry maids, all together with precision drill.

'Do you enjoy our May Day Parade?' Joe looked round to find the entertainments officer at his side. 'Ve heff more Russian culture for you today, Nina Provokovitch, an opera singer. Have you heard of her?' Joe shook his head. 'Nina will sing aria in praise of the Kiev Workers Collective who completed 1500 tractors in one day.'

'Y'know,' said Mavis in her informative voice three days later while Joe was sipping his morning tea, 'we're not getting any nearer Las Palmas.'

'What makes you think that, old girl?' She went across to the cabin window and pulled aside the curtain. 'That for instance.' Joe looked out. The swimming pool had frozen over. 'And another thing,' she continued. 'All this gunfire we keep hearing, these rockets and planes and helicopters. Not the normal sort of thing you get on a cruise.' Joe didn't answer. He was looking out of the window.

'Marvellous, isn't it?' he said at length. 'Spend seven hundred quid on a holiday trip and end up shadowing the NATO fleet off Iceland.'

When Canadian news cameraman Bill Linn took delivery of his 24-foot cruiser he decided to do things in style and invited an attractive TV star to break a bottle of champagne over its bow. To keep glass fragments from flying, the bottle was bound with tape. The girl took seven swipes at the bow until someone suggested she tried the fairlead. She did. The guests were showered with aluminium fragments, while the bottle still hung there, intact.

A man jogging along the beach on the Pacific Island of Guam found a bottle with a note inside. It had been dropped in the Puget Sound some years previously and contained the following poem:

'If, by the time this reaches you, I am old and gray, I know that our love will be as fresh as it is today.'

'Bob'

The man forwarded the message to the *Seattle Times* who traced the addressee and read the poem over the phone. The woman listened then burst into laughter.

'That was my *dummy* husband,' she said. 'We're divorced now,' and hung up.

Mousehole

Mice have been at me again during the winter. They've made a hole in my rubber dinghy. Naturally, I am angry about it; who wouldn't be after all the trouble one goes to, dusting it down with baby powder and parcelling it away in the

'America? . . . Personally I think Vespuccia sounds better.'

shed? Still, as King Louis XVI is reported to have said as he gazed up at M Guillotine's new invention: 'I do applaud fine craftsmanship.' So it is with this mousehole.

If I had wanted to put a porthole in the side of the boat I couldn't have cut a neater, rounder hole. It is a perfect circle. One mouse must have scribed round doing the jaw work, while another one stood on his tail.

My wife is secretly pleased, of course. A typical 'modern', she is all for buying a new dinghy. It was the same when I came to her with a moth hole in my pullover; she never attempts to mend anything. And when I think of the hours my mother spent with her mushroom darning my father's socks! I'm glad my old mum taught me the virtue of making do. Of course, I shall repair it.

Keeping that dinghy going has become a crusade with me. How could I now abandon it after all we have been through together; old 'rumpled and crumpled', the only rubber dinghy left in the racks the night a gang went through the club stockade with a pantechnicon. The only rubber dinghy ever to have survived an attack by an Irish wolfhound. It's not just a friend, it's part of our family heritage. How could I ever face the children again with the knowledge that their paddling pool has gone to the dustmen. What gold-tinted memories will endure . . . teaching tortoise to swim underwater. You bet I shall have to repair it.

Either that, or I shall take it to the vulcanising centre. Although, come to think of it, they are not very inspiring. Last time I dragged it in, the man said they didn't handle disposals.

Unfortunately, although I am resolved to repair it, my skills don't match my determination. I'm not very good at patching. I used to be. The Cyclist Touring Club gave me a prize once for mending a bike puncture in under four minutes. But over the years the eyes have weakened, the fingers have thickened, and, anyway, can you still get a *John Bull* puncture outfit?

I missed out. I bought the dinghy at the first Beaulieu Boat Jumble and they never gave me a handbook. What a difference that would have made. I could have turned to the section marked maintenance and seen how one is supposed to go about patching. My own method goes something like this:

1. Drag inflatable to thistle-less patch of lawn and inflate.
2. Paint on Fairy Liquid. Watch as frothing begins.
3. Identify serious holes. Dry. Make chalk mark.
4. Deflate. Roughen up surface with sandpaper. Lose chalk mark.
5. Open tin of thrixotropic glue. Spread liberally. Giggle.
6. Apply second coat of thrixotropic glue. Giggle uncontrollably.
7. Sober up to find patch has been placed over letter box.

But there seems little chance of repairing the mouse damage, since the hole is about twice as large as the biggest patch supplied. My only hope is to cut away the entire bow section, dart the ends and bring them round to fashion a new bow. It means I shall be left with an inflatable just over 4 feet long. Unless . . . unless, by a happy coincidence some reader has a mousehole in his after end and we could arrange something to our mutual advantage.